FOR YOU...

How long will my love still remain?

Published in the UK in 2021 by Old Swan Press

Paperback ISBN 978-1-8384337-3-4
.epub eBook ISBN 978-1-8384337-4-1
.mobi eBook ISBN 978-1-8384337-5-8

Cover design and typeset by SpiffingCovers

FOR YOU...

How long will my love still remain?

A collection of poems

by

FRANK JONES

Frank Jones was born in Liverpool, in 1948, and now lives in Chester. His stage comedy It's Now or Never! was produced by the Chester Gateway Theatre, and his Christmas rock & roll pantomime Jumping Jack Flash by the Liverpool Everyman. His first novel Her Name Was Charlie is currently on sale. Apart from poetry and plays, he also enjoys writing children's stories (ages ranging from pre-school to mid-teen) and writes songs.

To my wife

Sarah Jones

1952 - 2009

CONTENTS

The poems are set out alphabetically, in categories which are also in alphabetical order.

Autobiographical

1959

They always seemed another race, from another time, another place. They

owned cars, lived in houses with gardens, had bathrooms, hot water. They wore

new clothes used forks and knives. Did all the things that their type do. Like

play tennis, eat food they paid cash for not got on the bill, 'til payday. Their

fathers went to work in clean shirts and came home in clean shirts. Not like his.

They went to work in shoes, not boots. They bought newspapers, like the Mail, the

Express, some even the Telegraph, the Times, not the Sketch or Mirror. They had

wardrobes in their bedrooms, lampshades, carpets on the floor not oilcloth. They

smoked coffin nails like Senior Service, Craven A, not Woodbines or rollies. They

didn't have bugs, fleas, cockroaches, mice. They ate suppers, before going to bed.

They had washing machines for their clothes, not the sink. They drank fresh milk

from the milkman, not sterry from Sammy's. They never got their gas meters robbed or windows smashed at midnight, with steel tubes wrapped in cotton wool.

They always seemed like another race from another time, another place, and now he

was among them. Walking, talking, watching their dexterity with a knife and fork at

dinnertime. Names attached to faces, friendships formed, jokes told, laughter shared

as each day passed, they became less and less another race, from another time, another

place. Bonds formed, yet no enemies. They took to him, his quiet nature, his wit, and sense

of tumour. He took to them, even the ones with names like Kenneth and Hugh and Shaun.

As the days turned to months, without realising it, he no longer felt like an outsider.

—

(Tuesday, 25th September 2018)

BOB

My dad fought in the war
On the south coast, with a big gun
Defending the cockneys from Hitler's mob
Shooting Nazis down must have been fun
I don't know how many he shot
Nobody kept any score
I hope he aimed better than when at the fair
Because most of his shots hit the floor

My dad fought in the war
And when the war came to an end
They gave him two medals and a 'bugger off' suit
There was nothing left to defend
So, he came back home to our house
To his daughter, his wife, and two boys
But, after five years of explosions and bombs
He couldn't get to sleep, for their noise

My dad fought in the war
Now, a hero without any cause
He was scrimping and scratching to find a job
Like a dog with a bone in its jaws
He spent all his days humping big sacks of coal
Every twenty sacks equalled a ton
He'd return home at night, exhausted and black
Wishing he was back there, on his gun

My dad fought in the war
But he wasn't the only one
A *'Land fit for Heroes,'* Lloyd George had once said
But when all that is said and done
Preserving the ways of the country they loved
Were just, normal blokes, doing their job
And now, they've all gone, including my dad,
My dad, with a name that was...
'Bob'.

—

(Saturday, 15th September 2018)

BOULEVARD MILL LANE

Trois o'clock on a Janvier morning
Accompanied by my mam's pain
My little world entered your big world
Bonjour Boulevade Mill Lane!
A big brass bed in the parlour
Became my stop-off point
Bob and Lizzie's latest production
I hope, I didn't disappoint

Quatre in a line of quatre
Neuf years between me and number three
Trois years after the war
I was planned – *obviously*
But somehow, we all managed
Tightrope-walking the poverty line
Fine-dining chips and scouse and porridge
Washed down with Camelia wine

In our fifteen-bedroomed chateau
All mod-cons: we had none
A two-up, two down terraced
With wildlife – just for fun
Remembering all those distant days
In our non-gargantuan home
Days of Sunlight soap and darned socks
And, of course, a nit-nurse comb

No hot water (except for kettles)
On Mill Lane boulevard
The only light from a gas mantle
With le pissoire, down le yard
Oilcloth covering all the floors
Bedrooms cold as ice
And definitely no telly or phone
Just hot and cold running mice

And now, the Jaguar's parked on the drive
Of my four-bedroom detached
In an up-market district of Chester
Where cups and saucers match
My mam and dad would be proud of me –
At least, I like to think

"Hey, mam, come and have a look at this!
It's stainless-steel, that sink!
There's two inside bogs
A five-ringed hob
And two sets of bisexual doors
That's not real wood, you're standing on -
They're laminated floors"

So, it must be true, as the saying goes
And, boy, does it make me glad
You can take the lad out of Liverpool
But not the Liverpool out of the lad.

(Tuesday, 18th September 2018)

BROKEN MAN

I try to be
The best that I can be
I try to see
The good inside of me
But when in doubt
And shadows smother me
With ghosts of past lives haunting me
I realise, as far as I can see
I'm just, a broken man.

And when I joke
And play the clown
With friends and loved ones
Loving me
Deep down inside
I cannot hide
Beneath it all
Behind the mask
I'm just, a broken man

Maybe one day
I'll find a way
To break free from these chains
These chains surrounding me
Binding me
From the man that I should be
Blinding me
Reminding me
I'm just, a broken man

Where did I go wrong?
How did I play along?
What happened to that little boy
Of so long ago
Who grew to be the man
Who does the best he can
Yet deep inside
He cannot hide
He's just, a broken man

I try to be
The best that I can be
I try to see
The good inside of me
But when in doubt
And shadows smother me
With ghosts of past lives haunting me
I realise, as far as I can see
I'm still that broken man.

—

(1st August 2018)

CATABLANCA
(THE OLD MAN AND THE KITTEN)

"Of all the gin joints in all the towns in all the world
you walked into mine"

I know you'll break my heart
When it's time for you to go
(or maybe I'll go first)
But let's just put that thought away
And think about tomorrow and today
Of happy times,
The times yet still to come

"I think this is the beginning of a beautiful friendship"

Of times of mischief, cheekiness, and fun
We two, together, scoundrels on the run
Like Butch and Sundance
You and me, against the world
New chapters of our lives to be unfurled
Your sunrise, my sunset, hand in hand
It doesn't take a lot to understand
It doesn't take much work to make it fit
Just you and me together, so...

"Here's looking at you, kit"

—

(Sunday, 27th September 2020)

GONE

My love I send you, like tiny falling raindrops, landing on your heart
My love I send you, like stars, to light up the dark and guide my way to you
My love I send you, like a million forget-me-nots, so you will always remember

For I cannot forget.

You brought a song to my life. You were the music of my soul.
You were the sunshine in my mind. You brought beauty to my thoughts.
You brought warmth to my chill. You were the laughter in my sorrow.
You brought the breeze that dried my tears

Rest In Peace

—

(1st part circa 2013, 2nd part 2018. Combined into one poem: 2018)

GORILLA

I'm walking along the towpath of the Shropshire Union
He's ambling ahead of me; twenty-five yards
Slowly
slower than me:
a gorilla

Straggly greasy hair
scruffy biker jacket Jeans
Rough and broad as a brick shithouse
Unsavoury
No one else around
just him and me

I'm in a hurry for my appointment
Consternation clouds my mind
He's ambling ahead of me
fifteen-twenty yards
Slowly
slower than me:
a gorilla

I'm gaining on him.
I slow down
But I can't slow down I need to hurry
I need to hurry, or I'll be late

Straggly greasy hair
scruffy biker jacket, jeans
Broad and rough as a brick shithouse
Unsavoury

No one else around
just him and me

I'm at his mercy
at his mercy
He's ambling ahead of me; ten-fifteen yards
Slowly
slower than me:
a gorilla

Should I tempt fate and rush past?
How easy would it be for him
To mug me and throw me in the canal

I can't swim I can't swim I'd drown
'BODY FISHED OUT OF CANAL'
For the sake of seven pound

Straggly greasy hair
scruffy biker jacket Jeans
Broad and rough as a brick shithouse
Unsavoury
No one else around
just him and me
Straggly greasy hair
scruffy biker jacket Jeans
Broad and rough as a brick shithouse
Unsavoury
No one else around
just him and me

I'm gaining on him.

For You...

I slow down
But I can't slow down I need to hurry
I need to hurry, or I'll be late

I need to make a decision
Indecision stifles my mind
He's ambling ahead of me; five-ten yards
Slowly
slower than me:
a gorilla

Suddenly he stops turns, and looks into the canal
My chance has come I increase my step
As I approach him to pass, he looks at me

I look at him as he smiles and points
Down at the water my eyes follow the direction
A mother duck with her nine, squabbling offspring

'They're luvly, aren't they...?' he says quietly, gently, to me
How could I not agree, as we share a smile
'I saw a moorhen, yesterday...' he continues with a hint of pride

For a moment... two strangers, side by side on a towpath
Are united as they admire a snapshot of nature
The first stranger:
a gorilla
the second stranger:
A TWAT

——

(Monday, 16th March 2020)

I CONFESS

(St. Oswald's, Old Swan, 1955)

"Bless me Father, for I have sinned
This is my first confession"

Lined up in the pews of the whispering church
Boys to the left, girls to the right
Like lambs to the slaughter, we knelt in prayer
Preparing to 'fight the good fight'

Stern-looking teachers like butch prison guards
Controlling us all with a stare
Then the door opens, the first one went in
Stale frankincense filling the air

Parents in debt for our navy-blue suits
Exposed knees knocking with fear
Wearing blue satin sashes and medals of tin
Done up in our de-rigueur gear

Across the church, on the opposite side
The girls, each one dressed like an angel
All queueing up, to confess their sins
Sins? Jesus Christ – we were seven.

Oh, yes, I forgot – Original Sin
Committed by Adam and Eve
So, why do we have to carry the can?
For those two – would you believe?
Then my turn came to walk through the door
Trembling, I twisted the knob

I walked in, knelt down, stared at the curtain
Then said, almost with a sob...

"Bless me Father, for I have sinned
This is my first confession"

I couldn't think of anything, I'd done in my life
To mark me down as a *'sinner'*
So, started to conjure up little-boy fibs
I needed to sound like a winner...

'I forgot all the prayers I'm supposed to say
Morning, noon, and night,
And grace before, and after, my meals'
(Jesus Christ – what a load of *shite!*)

'I gave old buck to me mam and dad'
(Old Uncle Tom Cobley an' all)
And after a minute of boring the priest
I swear I could hear him yawn

My Act of Contrition was next in line
I spurted it out with some zest
A perfect rendition, word for word
Relieved it was then off my chest

He gave me 'absolution' (whatever that was)
I think it meant letting me off
Then next came my penance – he took a deep breath
Then he said, with a smoker's cough:

'Say three Hail Marys and three Our Fathers
And be sure to be a good boy'
'Thank you, father,' I sheepishly said
But felt it had all been a ploy

Because...
Outside of the box, I knelt in prayer
My three Hail Marys to say
'Hail Mary, full of gas...
The Lord is with Thee...
Blessed art Thou, a monk swimmin'...'

—

(Sunday, 16th September 2018)

MICROCOSM

When I was a younger man
I had more time than I could need
Yet not that much to say
And now that I'm an older man
A million words locked in my heart
Stay silent as time drifts away

When I was a younger man
My breast bore boundless love for her
Who turned her back on my embrace
And now that I'm an older man
My love for her exists no more:
Her memory, a faded grace

When I was a younger man
There was no target that I feared
There was no goal that left me fazed
And now that I'm an older man
Life's marathon has run its course
All ambitions now erased

When I was a younger man
Beyond the stars my daydreams flew
Each one in its naive prime
And now that I'm an older man
Those broken dreams lie gathering dust
In the distant gutter of time

—

(Thursday, 20th September 2018)

MR LONELY

Mr Lonely sits in his chair
Surrounded by no-one for nobody's there
As the morning gives birth to the rest of the day
As the rest of the world are at work or at play
Mr Lonely sits in his chair
Surrounded by no-one for nobody's there

Like a condemned man that sits in the dock
Mr Lonely's condemned to the tick of the clock
And the sound of the rain on the window's face
And the beat of his heart as his memories race

Mr Lonely sits in his chair
Remembering times that used to be there
As the evening's yawn gives birth to the night
As the curtains are drawn to the sodium light
Mr Lonely climbs up the stairs
Remembering times that used to be theirs

—

(Sunday, 30th January 2011)

PEGASUS HERO

From the day I was born
You have always been there
Through thick and through thin
You have always been there
Never the flash, never the brash
Just the comforting feel of sausage and mash
You have always been there

Since I took my first steps
You have always been there
Through dark times and light
You have always been there
Never to judge, never to budge
Never the one to bear a grudge
You have always been there

When life knocked me down
You have always been there
Then knocked down again
And still you were there
As night followed day
As tears followed play
You have always been there
My Pegasus hero who remains unsung
Avoiding the plinth where you belong
All the way through, my hair-brained schemes
All the way through, my impossible dreams
You have always been there
For me

———

Written to celebrate the 80th birthday of my brother, Kenny – ex paratrooper.

(Fran. Wednesday, 27th July 2016)

POEMS

Not by the dozens, not by the tens, nor the quadruplets
just by the ones. Ones. Few and far between. Heartfelt.
Sincere. To raise a glass, to raise a tear, to raise a laugh,
to touch peoples' hearts, emotions, thought processes.

From mine to yours, yours to where? Swirling, floating,
released to the air, moving around, up and down, in and out
A pebble into a lake, ripples spreading outwards. Autumn leaves
blown down from the trees. Caught by the wind, tossing and

turning; free flight. Spreading for miles before landing where?
Somewhere? Nowhere? Upstairs, downstairs, in Milady's chamber?
He breathes life into his cupped hands then spreads his palms and it flies
taking off: a fledgling bird into the unknown. Will it survive? Nature is cruel.

Writing is worse.

—

(Monday, 22nd October 2018)

SCRAMBLED EGGS

Scrambled slowly, omelettes quickly, she'd told him in the past, so there he

was preparing the pan for scrambled. He lit the gas, poured in a slug of cow

juice followed by a mini Mont Blanc of anchor then turned up the flame.

Beating two eggs in a mug, he watched the butter losing its battle to stay

independent as it dissolved into a mini island of defiance, surrounded by a

sea of white. He eased the eggs into the pan and began to stir with the old

wooden spoon he used for preparing cous-cous for the breeding sparrow chicks.

Be patient lads – you're next. Slowly, slowly, curving the spoon, stirring the eggs

then clipping the sliced ham with the scissors, letting it drop into the mixture.

Scooping it out onto the toast then grinding on the black pepper, it was ready to

take upstairs. As he entered the room she was sitting up in the bed, reading her book.

'Thanks, love,' she said, as he placed the tray onto her lap. He lay on the bed beside her

And gazed up at the ceiling. The Sunday morning sunshine painted the room gold. 'Thanks

for looking after me,' she said, as she ate her breakfast. 'You look after me, don't you?

It's a team effort,' he replied. Half a minute passed in silence, then out of the blue she said,

'If anything happens to me, will you promise to look after David?' 'Of course, I'll look after

David. He's my son, isn't he?' he replied, thinking it a strange request. She didn't mention

Michael. Within twelve months, as fingers of fading sun pierced the evening rain clouds, he

scattered her ashes onto Coniston then watched, with David and Michael, two sunflower

heads, side by side, assisted by a breeze, floating out into the lake toward her beloved

Wildcat Island.

—

(Saturday 6th October 2018)

THE MAN WHO NEARLY WAS

What time is the next bus to fame and fortune?
I missed the last one
I must have been in the lavatory
When it came, and then was gone
Or I might have been out shopping
For something no-one needs
Like a paperweight, a butter knife
Or, another pet to feed

I might have been in the right place
But not at the right time
Or possibly the wrong place
Thinking I was doing fine
So, I waited, and I waited
Writing musicals, plays and rhyme
Yes, it *was* the right place
But just at the wrong time

So, when you reach the ivory towers
Just don't get too excited
You can bet your bottom dollar
Someone else will be delighted
And you'll end up on your hands and knees
Licking crumbs up off the floor
Then, when the crumbs have disappeared
They'll show you to the door.

Three score years and ten they say
That's your innings – now you're out
Even though there's plenty more to come

They think you've lost your clout
Success is obviously rationed
To the specially chosen few
I could have been a contender
But was at the back of the queue

And now, it's suddenly dawned on me
How I came to miss that bus
And now I feel the guilty one
For kicking up this fuss
I was working inside factories
Doing sixty hours a week
Arriving home exhausted
Have my tea then fall asleep

Mortgage to pay, family to feed
Car to keep on the road
My life going 'round, in circles
My brain was in overload
And now looking back with hindsight
It's so clear for me to see
That imaginary bus just didn't exist
It was never meant to be

——

(Sunday, 16th September 2018)

FORD'S
(WHEN THE BELL RANG)

We came
Gushing out
Like a torrent
A torrent of humanity.
Toward the exit door.
As the rivulets raced from each clocking station, we made our way down alleyways and passages, converging as we went, into bigger, stronger flows. Taking shortcuts through
machine sections.
Gathering pace.
Our urgency disproportionate to our final goal.
Released from our shackles.
We surged, towards the fresh air.
The daylight.
Elated by freedom.
We came,
Flowing out
like a dropped vase,
Shattered into hundreds of shards.
Each one unique.
Each one the same.
Into the car park.
Anxious feet pounding
Got to be first: onto the scooter.
Got to be first: into the car.
Got to be first: onto the bike.
Got to be first: to cross to the bus stop.
Through the main gate.
Spewing out.

A wave of molten humanity, erupting from the mouth of the factory.
Gathering pace.
Unstoppable.
Our urgency disproportionate to our final goal.
Freedom
Freedom
Freedom...
Until tomorrow

——

(Circa: 2010)

An extract set out as a poem, from my novel, 'Her Name Was Charlie'.

Children

DINKAPOOS

Ten excited Dinkapoos, hopping down the street
Diddy did a somersault and injured both his feet

Nine happy Dinkapoos, climbing up the Hode
Granny Dunka Dinkapoo slipped upon a toad

Eight cheerful Dinkapoos, skipping 'round the crescent
Little Lottie Dinkapoo disturbed an angry pheasant

Seven smiling Dinkapoos, jogging down the lane
Great Grandad Dongle Dinkapoo prefers to go by train

Six laughing Dinkapoos, splashing in the sea
Baby Nellie Dinkapoo has a nappy full of wee!

Five serious Dinkapoos, sailing on the lake
Pippy Peanut banged his head, and it began to ache

Four tired Dinkapoos, trudging down the track
Aunty stops to tie her lace, and sits upon a tack

Three angry Dinkapoos, along the promenade
Silly Sausage Dinkapoo went down the boulevard

Two dozy Dinkapoos, creeping through the dark
Nooky woke a sleeping dog and it began to bark
One lonely Dinkapoo – no more to be said
Searching for the other nine, who have all gone home
To bed!

(Friday, 7th July 1995)

DISRAELI POLLOP

Disraeli Pollop walked with a run
He lived in a square house that was round
He was six feet three at the front
And three feet six at the back
His goldfish lived in a cage
And his budgie could swim
His mother was his father
And his father was his mother
He thought carrots were bananas
And couldn't understand why they were so hard to bite

He was once banned from a funeral for singing:
"Happy Deathday, to you
Happy Deathday to you
The grave is now open
It's goodbye to you"
It was his granny's funeral

He thought mustard was custard
And put it on his jelly
He thought up was down and down was up
And couldn't understand
Why his table and chairs kept falling off the ceiling

He once cooked his Christmas dinner in his washing machine
And it came out – Christmas soup
He put a sprig of holly on top, and ate it with his dog
Then when he'd finished eating his dog
He ate his cat for afters
One day he slipped on a matchstick

Fell head-first into a steaming great dollop
And that was the end of Disraeli Pollop.

—

(Sunday, 13th August 2017)

GRANDPA GRUMP

Grandpa Grump did a silly thing last week.
He tried to lift a heavy box then slipped and couldn't speak.
He screeched out with fright and fell to the floor.
Just as a knock came at the front door.

So, grandma left grandpa stretched out on the mat
In front of the fire, with the dog and the cat.
The milkman shouted, *'Ten pound-fifty.'*
Grandma paid the bill, then returned, quite nifty.

'Call me an ambulance - I'm three parts dead.'
'I'll just put the yeast in my homemade bread...'
Then into the kitchen grandma did totter
Leaving grandpa on carpet, getting hotter and hotter

'Right now, where were we?' grandma returned.
'Shift me from fire, I've almost burned.'
'Right kids,' said grandma, *'put down your toys.'*
But no-one could hear her, above all the noise.

'Have you lot gone deaf?' poor grandpa then roared,
Not taking too kindly, to being ignored
So, I took his head and gran took his knees,
And there was our grandpa beginning to wheeze.

Huffing and puffing, with a cough and a splutter.
Staring up at the ceiling, he'd started to mutter.
I pulled him up, as gran pulled him down.
'You'll snap me in half,' he screamed with a frown.

He moaned and he groaned and started to gripe,
Then gave out a squeal as he rolled on his pipe.
And it broke in two and stuck in his bum,
While he's banging on, with a mouth like a drum.

And all this 'cos grandpa tried liftin' a box,
Without any slippers – just wearing his socks.
And there was us all, trying hard not to giggle,
As we looked at our grandpa, who'd started to wriggle,

To try and turn 'round, move his face from the fire.
He was doing his best, but he'd started to tire.
His face and his neck were all covered in sweat
And his armpits had all gone stinky and wet.

'Right kids!' said grandma, *'Let's all do our best!'*
So, we gathered 'round grandpa, me and the rest.
'When I shout 'THREE! - push as hard as can.'
As she tried not to laugh, *'THREE!'* shouted gran.

We all grabbed grandpa as best as we could.
He was old but was heavy – like a dead lump of wood.
We heaved, and we pushed, and we shoved him over.
We shifted the cat and we chased out Rover.

In rushed Aunt Ethel, with two, big, white pills.
'Swallow these, dad, they're for coughs, colds and chills.'
'How can I swallow them, you silly, daft daughter?
You've fetched me the pills, but not brung any water.'

My brother, Bertie, had a super plan.
He ran into garden shed, to find the watering can.

Gran went to kitchen, to fetch him a cup.
Bertie reappeared, *'Here y'are, grandpa, sup up!'*

But just when he thought there was a change in his luck
Bertie slipped on Rover's bone - poor grandpa's head got stuck.
He growled and he shouted. He grunted and cussed.
We heaved and we pulled, and we twisted and pushed.

'It's no use, I'm stuck fast,' came a squeak from the spout.
'Send for the police. Get fire brigade out.'
'Have you no common sense?' retorted my gran.
'They'll not send a fire engine, for your head, in a can.'

'Well, you'll have to do summat,' he continued to bark.
'Cos, I'm covered in sweat, and I don't like this dark.'
So, we all stood and pondered on what to do next,
As grandpa got sweatier, flummoxed and vexed.

'I've made a decision,' winked grandma, to me.
'We'll think this one out - with a nice, pot of tea.'
'How can I sup tea - the state as I'm in?'
'I'm not talking to you!' snarled gran, with a grin.

So, into the kitchen the gang of us trooped,
Leaving grandpa on cushions, all flustered and drooped.
There was home-made cakes and biscuits galore.
'Eat as much as you can,' smiled gran, *'while I pour.'*
We had such a grand time, that we almost forgot,
poor grandpa, in parlour, all sweaty and hot.

Half an hour later - I thought it was weird.
I took him a doughnut, and there he was - disappeared.

We searched high and low, from cellar to loft.
We looked and we listened - not a sneeze, not a cough.

For nowhere did grandpa appear to be found.
'That's queer,' counted grandma... 'Milkman owes me a pound.'

—

(Originally, circa 1994 + additional verses added September 2018)

I WISH I WAS A BLACKBIRD

I wish, I was a blackbird
Flying from bush to bush
It's a beautiful bird, the blackbird
Did you know, it's a type of thrush?
You see them in parks and gardens
And sometimes you see them in town
But only the male blackbird is black
The female blackbird is brown

I wish I was a blackbird
With my peaceful, relaxing song
Drifting down from the trees and rooftops
To the humans as they walk along
And each evening when I feel hungry
Eating snails... worms... and slugs... for tea...
Never again... my fish fingers and chips
On second thoughts - I'll keep being ME!

(Saturday, 27th June 2020)

LITTLE CHIFFCHAFF, SITTING UP IN THE TREE

Little chiffchaff sitting up in the tree
Why d'you want to build your nest with me?
Flying all the way across the sea
From Africa.
Little Chiffchaff on the washing line
Why d'you want to leave your world behind?
Flying all the way across to mine
From Africa.
If you were a waxwing
Or a hoopoe
If you were an oriole
Don't you just know
People everywhere would stand and stare
In great surprise, not believe their eyes
But we know, deep down inside, you'll always be
Just a little chiffchaff sitting up in the apple tree
Just a little green bird - there for us to see
Just a little chiffchaff – singing his song for me...

"Chiff-chaff, chiff-chaff, chiff-chaff, chiff-chaff."

(Written circa 1980, for my children, on seeing a chiffchaff in the back garden)

LITTLE DAISY DINKLE

Little Daisy Dinkle
Had a salty twinkle
Right in the corner of her eye
She visited the doctor
But the doctor locked her
Up with the pigs in the sty

The pigs took exception
To Daisy's reflection
That stared at them out of the mud
They grunted and shouted
Snorted and snouted
Then rang Priory Bell for M'lud

M'lud did arrive
With a buzzing beehive
Fixed firm to the top of his head
He sneezed and he wheezed
And was greatly displeased
At the price of a slice of fried bread

"*What a terrible fuss,*" M'lud did cuss
As the bees on his knees lost their temper
Then the hogs from the bogs
With a barrow of logs
Bumped him into a vat of distemper
With an almighty *SPLASH!*
M'lud wore his sash

From his nose to the tip of his ear
As the distemper settled
The little pig fettled
A firkin of green ginger beer

Drink up, one and all
For it's only a squall
Smiled M'lud as the bees and pigs gloated
Then they clambered aboard
Slashed the rope with a sword
And away in the melon boat floated

Little Daisy Dinkle
Had a sadly twinkle
At the prospect of being alone
She shouted and waved
And hoped to be saved
By the use her carrot-shaped phone

M'lud said "Hello?"
As a pig chewed his toe
And the buzzling bees drove him quite crazy
For the price of a pound
The boat turned around
Then steered a course back toward Daisy.

Little Daisy did smile
When in a short while
The melon boat drew up beside her
She clambered aboard
As the big pig snored
Having guzzled a gobbin* of cider

The boat sailed away
For the rest of the day
'Cross an ocean of chocolate ice cream
Then Daisy did blink
And with a short think
Realised it had all been a dream

*to find the quantity of a gobbin, simply add two squiffles and a pog together.

—

(Sunday 6th October 1996)

LITTLE ERIC'S DRIVING TEST

Little Eric was thrilled. He rushed up to his dad and said excitedly, 'Dad! Dad! I want to learn to drive a car!' His dad's big eyes bulged even bigger. 'Don't talk silly,' he said, to Eric. 'Your legs are too short. You'd never reach the pedals.' Little Eric felt glum, but he wasn't put off his idea. He rushed up to his mum and said joyfully, 'Mum! Mum! I want to learn to drive a car!' His mum grinned, showing her crooked teeth, and said, 'Don't talk silly, your arms are too short. You'd never reach the steering wheel.' Little Eric felt glum, but he wasn't put off his idea. Next day he rushed up to his teacher, and said happily, 'Miss Bogroll, I want to learn to drive a car!' Miss Bogroll laughed so much the tears ran down her leathery cheeks.

Little Eric felt glum. He was about to give up on the idea when he told his gran. 'What a great idea!' she said. 'Good for you!' So, he saved up all his pocket money. He saved and saved, until he had enough money for some driving lessons. He took the driving lessons and, after some time, took his driving test. He failed. He saved and saved again then took more lessons and failed. Then, he took even more lessons and kept on failing. His dad, mum, and Miss Bogroll all told him to give up on his silly idea. But his gran said, 'Never give up, Eric,' and she gave him some money. Eric had more driving lessons, and was about to take his driving test again. He thought to himself, 'If I fail this time - I'll give up.'

It was his last chance to learn how to drive. After forty minutes of his driving test, he stopped the car. The driving test examiner turned his miserable face to Eric. '*Oh, no. I've failed again,*' thought Eric. Then, in his most miserable voice, the examiner said, *'I'm pleased to tell you, you've passed.'* Eric and his gran were thrilled to bits. *'Impossible!'* said his dad. *'I can't believe it!'* said his mum. Miss Bogroll, in a daze, stood with her mouth open, as a little bird jumped in and started picking bits of food from between her teeth. The following Friday though, they all believed it when on the front page of the newspaper, in big headlines, it said, *'Eric passes! – the first time in history a driving test has been passed by a crocodile!'*

—

(Thursday, 2nd April 2020)

LITTLE BIG TOES

There once was a woman
With little big toes
Growing out of the front of her feet
All the other toes
Were longer than those
Making those little big toes look sweet
But nobody knows
Why those little big toes
Chose as they did, not to grow
To a longer length than the other small toes
They just made up their mind and did so.

—

(Saturday, 23rd March 2019)

MR WOODMOUSE

With his overlarge ears
And his blackberry eyes
And his cute twitching nose
And his sandy brown coat
And his white underside
And his long slim tail
On four delicate feet
He trots along

Not for him
To shove and push
To streak and rush
Inelegant
Indelicate
As a house mouse would

You're quite right, he agreed

I have overlarge ears
I have blackberry eyes
And a cute twitching nose
And a sandy brown coat
With my white underside
And my long slim tail
On my delicate feet
With my courteous manners
I trot along
I'm the gentleman of the mouse world...
Ha! that's what he thinks...
Signed: A Dormouse.

What a load of nonsense from the pair of them.
Signed: A House mouse.

Heh! Heh! Heh! Fools!
Signed: A Harvest mouse.

—

(Monday, 23rd March 2020)

NIGHT, NIGHT

Time for bed, sleepy head
Time to close your eyes
Mr Sun has gone to bed
Mrs Moon is in the sky
Time for bed, sleepy head
Time to say night, night
In the darkness of the sky
The stars are shiny bright
Time for bed, sleepy head
Time to go to sleep
Mr Owl is out to play
Close your eyes, now, do not peep
Time for bed, sleepy head
Time to have sweet dreams
Til Mrs Morning brings the warmth
Of Mr Sun's sunbeams.
Time for bed, sleepy head
Time to drift away
Into the land of lullabies
To watch the fairies play

It's time to say night, night
Night, night, sweetheart
Night, night.

—

(Saturday 2nd March 2019)

A CHILD'S GUIDE TO THE SCIENCE OF SCAMOPOLOGY

(As explained by the left dishonourable, Professor Sicnarf Senoj).

A SKISH: is a cross between a skunk and a fish; it's an excellent swimmer, but it doesn't half stink.

AN ELEPOTAPHANTAMOUSE: nobody's knows what these are a cross between, because nobody's caught one, yet.

DID YOU REALISE: that 'ad' is the only word in the English language that begins and ends with the letters **a** + **d**? And that 'help' is the only four-letter word that is spelt by combining the letter **h** + **e** + **l** + **p** in that order?

DID YOU KNOW: that Wales is the only country in the United Kingdom that's actually in Wales.

A GRAN: is a cross between a grape and a pan - when they're young they're plump and juicy, but when they get old, they dry out, shrivel up, and drop out of your socks.

DID YOU REALISE: that there are no apples in a barrel of grapes.

STRANGE BUT TURE: it's not possible for a man to walk a fortnight (unless he waits for a bus).

A GRANDAD: is a cross between a grand piano and a lazy lad; they don't move very fast, but have a brilliant set of teeth.

DID YOU REALISE: that Her Majesty, Queen Elizabeth the

Second, started out life as a baby.

IF YOU WANT: to spell the word 'dog', start with the word 'doodlepug' then take out the 'odlepu' from the middle (a doodlepup is a baby doodlepug, and a doodlebog is a doodlepup with a sloppy bum).

IF YOU FITTED: a chimney pot to a tree, there would still be no smoke.

DID YOU REALISE: that England is one of only three countries in the United Kingdom that isn't in Scotland.

DID YOU KNOW: that Ireland has a larger collection of Irish grass than any other country in the world.

STRANGE BUT TRUE: there are hundreds of women living on the Isle of Man.

DID YOU KNOW: a duck can't cluck, and a chicken can't quack (chickens can't swim, either).

DID YOU REALISE: That, if you took every apple you've ever eaten, since you were a baby, and piled them up, in a big, pyramid-shaped hill, you still wouldn't be able to run as fast as a cat.

SNIGGLEPUG AND THE SEVELTEN PAPPERS

Time upon a once, Snigglepug slived in the pillage of Pillapock on the Lanks of the Miver Rersey. She was quit big for a Poggle, from the nips of her tops, to the tips of her pops she was almost three centimops lop.

One aftersoon in the piddle of the might, Snigglepug lecided to walk for a go. Down, down she loated. Down, down, until she meached the lop of the learest pupple.

"Grand Marnier!" houted Snigglepug, wit mucle frat, "Much how for sevelten pappers?" The giant, snug-nosed ratter gig Snigglepug a stare of great propoptions.

"Humungous pharht," he smigged wit great irritators.

"Humungous phart?" snuffed Snigglepug wit reat misdelief, "I'g lever neen so overpharted in my slife.

"Lake it or teave it," said the irruptious ratter, wit a snurf of conbaption.

"Merry thankyiou vuch," snilled Snigglepug wit a woff of reat snag unction.

"Ucan stuffit ho - up rite ur jaxy!"

"Werry vell," puffed the giant, snug-nosed ratter, "ginormous poop, then."

"Ginormous poop?" snuffed Snigglepug wit egen reater misdelief. The giant, snug-nosed ratter closed hig pyes, ang grumpled wit grumpling plump.

"Twelev... rof smellington willie."

"Smellington willie?" snarfed Snigglepug, "rof twelev?"

"Lastest of offres." snarfed the ratter, wit egen greater grumpling.

Suddeliest, Higglenog the Snoggle's arrivest led much to a snonk hooking of ledight frog the giant, snug-nosed ratter, for much hablebeen higs lostest of heldlong glove for her scute attenshet. Her was known threeout the urbanites of Pillapock as the Snoggle of amblest proportionate ang most ledicious whiffingham. Lusp, her capabilitong to run, leadst unto her championsting the firstest lace in the marathona rhase fron Pillapock to Little Piddling inde Pot. Higglenog's blatting of pyelids ang spouting of pips sont ratter ingu a wooning of smyriadical proportionest.

"Wittest how?" lurfed Higglenog to Snigglepug.

"Wittest how?" snarfed Snigglepug. "Ratter's robbety! Hat's wittest how!"A smuch hupping ang pupping frog snug-nosed ratter, saw follwed wit muckle blushting of cheleks in barrassment of truthings.

"Sevelten pappers - Humungous phart!" snuffed Snigglepug.

"Humungous phart - rof sevelten pappers?" glinst Higglenog.

"Smellington willie rof twelve!" overstuffed Snigglepug wit fractious punction. Higglehog the Snoggle lurned ot ratter, "wittest how, ratter robberty?" Snug-nosed ratter muckle stinkings inde skull...

"Ma, Ma, Ma!" ratter chukled wit gleeness of muckle. " Sily Snigglepug," he baffed. "Mullest of jokeling! Sevelten pappers - Smellington willie!"

"Muckle bester - sevelten pappers - bumtiddlybumpum."

Snug-nosed ratter turn grreenest mit sicklington. Higglenog batted pyelids ang spouting of pips...

"Sevelten pappers - bumtiddlybumpum," garked ratter, wit muckle garking.

"Weepiddlypeepoo!" snekkled Snigglepug wit grand packlewack.

Nater lhat tight, gy the slight of the slivery noom, Snigglepug ang Higglehog ab muckle of entertainymengs of Humpleton Pigglesnout, Mord Layor of Pillapock. Greatest feastling of sevelten pappers ang gravy, partuk. Snug-nosed ratter ment do bed wit mugglet of cocoa ang bok tittled, "Idliot's Guid Do Snoggles." ($&^ sword).

EHE TND.

STONE THE CROWS
(THE SCARECROW)

What a boring job
Standing here, day after day
Looking out across the field
Arms outstretched

What a rubbish job
Standing here, day after day
Gazing out across the field
Stupid hat, flapping coat

What a useless job
Standing here, day after day
Staring out across the field
Watching the birds eat their fill

What a poo job
Turnip for a head, carrot for a nose
Standing here, day after day
Being laughed at by crows

If I had any feet, they'd be freezing

—

(10.30am Saturday, 9th February 2019)

THE GOLDEN AGE

(I'd love to hear this recited by a class of primary schoolkids)

Thssssssssssssssssssssssssssssssssssssss

huff…

huff… huff…

huff… huff…
huff… huff…

huff… huff… huff… huff - huff… huff… huff… huff
huff… huff… huff… huff - huff… huff… huff… huff

huff, huff, huff, huff - huff, huff, huff, huff
huff, huff, huff, huff - huff, huff, huff, huff

huffhuffhuffhuff, huffhuffhuffhuff – huffhuffhuffhuff, huffhuffhuffhuff –
fuffuffuffuff fuffuffuffuff - fuffuffuffuff fuffuffuffuff - fuffuffuffuff fuffuffuffuff
(inside the carriages)
de dum, de dum – de dum, de dum – de dum, de dum – de dum, de dum
dedumdedum, dedumdedum, dedumdedum, dedumdedum,

d'dum d'dum, d'dum d'dum, d'dum d'dum, d'dum d'dum,
d'dum d'dum, d'dum d'dum, d'dum d'dum d'dum d'dum,

d'rumderum, d'rumderum, d'rumderum, d'rumderum,
d'rumderum, d'rumderum, d'rumderum, d'rumderum,

adiddledum adiddledum, adiddledum adiddledum,
adiddledum adiddledum, adiddledum adiddledum,
(the carriages are swaying)
altickleyebum altickleyebum, altickleyebum altickleyebum,
altickleyebum altickleyebum, altickleyebum altickleyebum,
(into the tunnel)
ohnoyouwon't, ohnoyouwon't, ohnoyouwon't, ohnoyouwon't,
ayesawill ayesawill, ayesawill ayesawill, ayesawill ayesawill,
ohnoyouwon't, ohnoyouwon't, ohnoyouwon't, ohnoyouwon't
(out of the tunnel)
altickleyebum altickleyebum, altickleyebum altickleyebum,
altickleyebum altickleyebum, altickleyebum altickleyebum,

adiddledum adiddledum, adiddledum adiddledum,
adiddledum adiddledum, adiddledum adiddledum,
(the whistle screams as the engine hits 100MPH)
adiddledum adiddledum, adiddledum adiddledum,
adiddledum adiddledum, adiddledum adiddledum,
(two hundred miles later)
altickleyebum altickleyebum, altickleyebum altickleyebum,
altickleyebum altickleyebum, altickleyebum altickleyebum,

fuffuffuffuff fuffuffuffuff - fuffuffuffuff fuffuffuffuff - fuffuffuffuff fuffuffuffuff
huffhuffhuffhuff, huffhuffhuffhuff – huffhuffhuffhuff, huffhuffhuffhuff –

huff, huff, huff, huff - huff, huff, huff, huff
huff, huff, huff, huff - huff, huff, huff, huff

huff... huff... huff... huff - huff... huff... huff... huff

huff... huff... huff... huff - huff... huff... huff... huff

huff... huff...
huff... huff...

huff... huff...

huff... huff...

huff...
(into Liverpool Lime Street station, the carriages creaking, brakes quietly squealing, as they followed their mistress under the smoke-stained canopy)

Thssssssssssssssssssssssssssssssssssssssss

Thssssssssssssssssssssssssssssssssssssssss

She creeps toward the buffers and gently kisses them as the journey comes to an end.
A twelve-year old boy jumps down from a carriage. His face is covered with delight and coal smuts. He has no way of knowing, but soon, all this will come to an end.
The end of an era:
the Golden Age, of Steam

—

(Thursday, 20th September 2018)

THE PRINCESS AND THE FROG

Once upon a time there lived a princess. She was beautiful. She dressed in the finest silk and lace, and she lived in a huge castle. She had servants to do everything for her, but there was one thing missing from her life: a handsome prince. This made her feel lonely. Each day she would walk the castle grounds, talking to the trees, the birds, the insects. One day, as she sat by the side of the pond, an ugly frog hopped out of the water and sat next to her. 'Why are you sad, beautiful princess?' croaked the ugly frog. She smiled, gently, then stood and walked back to the castle.

The next day, the same thing happened. 'Why are you sad, beautiful princess?' croaked the ugly frog. She reached down and, with a smile, gently stroked the frog on his head with her finger. Then she stood and walked back to the castle.

The third day came. 'Why are you sad, beautiful princess?' croaked the ugly frog. She reached down and held out her hand and the frog hopped onto her palm. She raised her hand to her face and said,

'All of my gold, my fine clothes, my castle, everything... I would leave them all behind, in exchange for a true friend, to share my life with. For all the riches in the world do not guarantee happiness.'

'Huh!' croaked the frog, snootily. 'But would you be prepared to leave behind your beauty...?'

'Of course,' she replied.

The frog could feel the sadness in her heart.

'And that is what you wish for, in all the world,' he croaked, 'a true friend?'

'Yes,' she replied.

The frog looked at her for a couple of seconds, then croaked, 'Raise me to your face...'

'Why...?' said the princess.

'I will become your friend, but first, you must kiss me...'

The princess laughed.

'Why would I want an ugly frog as a friend?'

'Kiss me...' croaked the frog, 'and you will find out...'

The princess laughed, again. 'You cheeky, little frog,' she said. 'You deserve a kiss for being so bold.' She raised her hand to her mouth and placed her lips onto the mouth of the frog, planting a gentle kiss. Then, something magical happened. The beautiful princess was no more, for she had turned into a lady frog.

'I am Prince Alan,' the frog said to her. 'Welcome, to my world.'

The lady frog looked at Prince Alan and saw how handsome he was. The sadness left her, and her heart was filled with a feeling of love. The two frogs hopped into the pond and swam away, to spend the rest of their lives together. The following year they had a family of five hundred wriggly tadpoles, who grew to be baby frogs, then, Prince Alan, his beautiful princess frog bride and all the little frogs lived hoppily ever after.

(Sunday, 16th February 2020)

THE ROBIN

I have a little Robin that comes into my garden every day.
He nibbles the food off the bird table, then hops down onto the lawn and gobbles up the insects.
I look at him and smile. He looks back at me, holds his head to one side and seems to smile back.
I sometimes offer him mealworms and he nervously hops towards me and eats them from my hand.
Then after one, maybe two, little poos on the lawn, he's off to next door.
He lives there with his mum, dad and two sisters.
His name is Robin Fellows and he's nine years old.
He's the weirdest kid I've ever seen.

—

Inspired by a real (feathered) robin that comes into my garden.

(Saturday 10th August 2019)

WELL KNOWN SLAYINGS:

Life begins at farty

A snitch in time slaves mine

Too many books soil the froth

Don't blow your own crumpet

Don't fudge a hook by its clover

A tool and his honey are soon farted

It's a pong road that has no gurning

There's no dutch thing as a free punch

Honey doesn't glow on trees

Man's best friend is a log…

(I'll have to get the wypetriter fixed.)

—

(Wednesday 19th February 2020)

YUM! YUM!

I had a little sausage dog
My granny named him 'Nipper'
I ate my little sausage dog
With custard and a kipper
Yum! Yum!

I found a ginger pussy cat
My grandad called her 'Poop'
I threw her in the Magimix
And then enjoyed Poop soup
Yum! Yum! Yum!

My uncle caught a fluffy bird
An Amazonian parrot
I stewed that little fluffy bird
With onions and a carrot
Yum! Yum! Yum! Yum!

My aunt bought me a special treat
A super, dappled pony
I found the biggest pan I could
For pony macaroni
Yum! Yum! Yum! Yum! Yum!

And when I went into the zoo
To bake a monkey cake
I sat and watched the monkeys play
It was a big mistake
For as the monkeys screamed and screeched
I wondered which to take

And while I made my mind up
I was swallowed by a snake
Yum! Yum!

—

(Tuesday, 8th October 1996)

Christmas

A SCALLYWAG'S CHRISTMAS

Descending from the midnight sky
Large snowflakes falling
Past the lamp like drunken moths
Float down in slow motion,
A white carpet forming
On the ground below:
My street in all her muffled majesty
As the snowflakes fall

A Morris Minor passes
Bonnet, roof and bootlid
Wear a thick white blanket
Spindly wipers slowly wiping,
Back wheels slippery sliding
Cautiously following the snail-like trail
Of those who went before
As the snowflakes fall

I sit within the darkened room
Gazing out - *excitidly excited!*
Net curtain draped behind my head
Wondering what Father Christmas
Will bring this time
My breath fogs the pane
And gradually the carpet thickens

As the snowflakes fall
White-hatted man with white tethered mongrel
Their nightly ritual now an expedition
Slowly leaving footprints in the snow

They pause, and the dog cocks its leg
On *My* lamppost – *My lamppost!*
All the time oblivious, not knowing
A scallywag has them in his sights
As the snowflakes fall

And then I climb into the bed
Onto the pillow plonk my head
And listen to the voices down below
Then up the stairs my mam will creep
I close my eyes, pretend to sleep
And all this time she still thinks I don't know
There is no Father Christmas
As the snowflakes fall.

—

(Thursday, 13th September 2018)

CHRISTMAS CHAOS!

(A Christmas song)

Intro: upbeat tempo, cascading Christmas bells etc.

CHORUS 1: Christmastime... Christmastime...
Let the bells of Christmas chime
Send their message, loud and clear:
Merry Christmas, a Happy New Year!

SPOKEN: But really – it's more like this...

VERSE 1: Grandma's on the sherry
Granddad's suppin' beer
Dad's gone down the boozer
Mother's feelin' queer
All the kids are whingein'
Their toys turned out all wrong
The cat's destroyed the tree – again!
Those sprouts – they don't 'alf pong!

SPOKEN: At –

CHORUS 2: Christmastime... Christmastime... (etc.)

SPOKEN: And, then –

VERSE 2: Uncle Billy's burpin'
Out the other end
Aunty Mary's singin'
Cos whisky's her best friend
All the kids are screamin'

Poor gran's gone for a nap
The pigs in blanket's are all burnt
Now, granddad's talking cr – rubbish

BRIDGE: It's that time of year again...
It's that time of year again...
It's that time of year again:

CHORUS 3: Christmastime... Christmastime...
Let the bells of Christmas chime
Send their message, loud and clear
Merry Christmas, a Happy New Year!

SHOUT: Altogether, now...

ALL REPEAT OUT CHORUS:

Christmastime... Christmastime...
Let the bells of Christmas chime
Send their message loud and clear
Merry Christmas, a Happy New Year...!
Merry Christmas, a Happy New Year...!
Merry Christmas...
A Happy...
New Year...!

(Outro: cascading Christmas bells.)

SHOUT: Merry Christmas, everyone...
Merry Christmas...
And a Happy New Year!

CLOSING WITH A SHOUT OF:

Mam! The dog's ate the leg off the turkey!

(Written in hospital, Wednesday 13th January 2016, while recovering from an operation for the removal of gall bladder)

CHRISTMAS COLOURS

White - like crystal snowflakes clinging to a bough

Blue - like shady daylight on an evening field of snow

Red - like shiny berries on a prickly holly tree

Gold - like merry laughter shared by you and me

Green - like twisted ivy seeking out its rambling course

Brown - like Christmas pudding as it sits in brandy sauce

Purple – like shiny wrapping on grandad's 'wool-rich' socks

Grey – like the face of the stiffened corpse as it lies in its cardboard box

—

(Wednesday, 4th December 2002)

CHRISTMASTIME

(A Christmas song)

Cascading hand bells intro...

CHORUS:

Christmastime, Christmastime
Let the bells of Christmas chime
Send their message, loud and clear
Merry Christmas, a Happy New Year

VERSE 1:

Once upon a Christmas
In a stable, far away
Mary had a baby boy
And lay him in the hay
A star was shining brightly
Its message was unfurled
That baby boy was sent to be
The saviour of our world

CHORUS:

Christmastime, Christmastime
Let the bells of Christmas chime
Send their message, loud and clear
Merry Christmas, a Happy New Year

VERSE 2:

Out across the desert
Following that star
The three wise men approaching
Had travelled from afar
For many days and many nights
Their precious gifts to bring
The baby lying in the hay
Jesus, King of Kings

CHORUS: Christmastime, Christmastime
Let the bells of Christmas chime
Send their message, loud and clear
Merry Christmas, a Happy New Year

REPEAT CHORUS TO END:
Christmastime, Christmastime
Let the bells of Christmas chime
Send their message, loud and clear
Merry Christmas, a Happy New Year

Merry Christmas, a Happy New Year...
Merry Christmas...
A Happy...
New Year

Cascading hand bells outro...

Merry Christmas, everyone!

—

(Written in 1983 and been in the cupboard ever since.)

HAPPY CHRISTMAS!

(northern accent)

'Twas on a Christmas evenin'
We were 'uddled 'round the fire
In the 'earth, a log wuz burnin'
Outside – a carol choir

The candles flickered 'round the room
We all sat there agog
Then, grandma's voice relieved the gloom
'By 'eck, have you seen this fog?'

The telly in the corner stood
Looking dark, depressed and lost
'Twas on that Christmas evenin'
That we counted up the cost

The turkey lay in the kitchen sink
Unloved, uncooked, unplucked
I swear I could smell it startin' t'stink
We h'ad nowt to eat, we were... starvin'

We 'ad nowt to eat that Christmas eve
Apart from cold, damp things
Like 'Princes' salmon spread butties
An' soggy onion rings

Still, it could have been much worse
Little Jimmy got 'is new bike
But I'll not f'get that Christmas
When the miners went on strike

(Circa December 2002)

THE MAGIC OF CHRISTMAS

(a Christmas song for children)

Verse 1:
The snowflakes are falling
The reindeer are calling
The bright lights are twinkling
For you and for me
The robins are singing
The church bells are ringing
The sleigh bells are tinkling
Our hearts are filled with glee

Verse 2:
The holly is laden
The mistletoe waiting
The candles are glowing
For you and for me
The log fire is gleaming
The children are dreaming
'til morning, not knowing
What lies beneath the tree

(musical interlude)

Bridge:
Then, during the night when all are asleep
Onto the rooftop he'll silently creep
As Rudolf and his friends are eating their hay
A red-suited man lifts a sack off his sleigh
Then slowly and surely as quiet as a mouse
The red-suited Santa will enter the house
To fill children's stockings with laughter and joy
The magic of Christmas for each girl and boy

Verse 3:
The snowflakes are falling
The reindeer are calling
And so, it continues
Again, and again
The robins are singing
The church bells are ringing
The magic of Christmas
Will always remain

—

(Sunday 10th December 2017)

Humorous

A BIT OF A NUISANCE

I'm a bit of a perfectionist
Her next door
Is a bit of a whinger
Him opposite
Is a bit of a footballer
My son
Is a bit of a guitarist
And my daughter
Is a bit of a gardener
My cousin
Is a bit of a writer
And my niece
Is a bit of an artist
The lad down the street
Is a bit of a birdwatcher
Uncle Bert
Is a bit of a singer
And Aunty Doris
Is a bit of a skater

And this poem
Is a bit of a nuisance

—

(Wednesday, 4th March 2020)

A LOSING BATTLE

Name a poem by John Betjeman
I don't know any
Not one?
No
Name a poem by Carol Anne Duffy
Who's she...?
What about Roger McGough?
Did he write poems as well?
As well as what?
Painting sunflowers
Ted Hughes...? Philip Larkin?
Never heard of them
Elliot?
Ness?
Let's go back a hundred years... Hopkins?
Silence of the Lambs...?
Kipling
That cake fella...?
Oh! For Christ's sake! You must know one poem by one poet!
Let me think... erm...
Well?
I said let me think...! erm... er... Got it!
At last... well...?
The Daffodils...
By...?
William...
Yes...?
Shakespeare

(Friday, 21st September 2018)

BIG SPENDER

Our beloved fuehrer, Boris,
appealing to us all,
as he proudly waved the invisible flag,
giving out his clarion call

"Eat out, to help out!
Eat out to help out!"

At the front of the queue,
inside the bank,
I'd made my decision
to empty the tank

"Eat out to help out!
Eat out to help out!"

I withdrew the whole lot,
my account now bare.
A spending spree beckoned
but I didn't care

"Eat out, to help out!
Eat out to help out!"

I marched through the door
for a gastronomic bash.
I didn't care less
about splashing all that cash

"Eat out, to help out!
Eat out to help out!"

Feeling ever so proud
of my patriotic guts
I then blew the whole lot on
a Kitkat,
a Penguin,
and a packet of Nobby's nuts.

—

(Written in the waiting room of the Elm treatment department, Clatterbridge Cancer Centre, Friday, 14th August 2020)

BROKEN

I have written 'Broken' to send a message to all lonely and despairing people throughout the world. That message is to never give up, no matter how dark your night is, no matter how long the tunnel. You are not alone. The Almighty Father will look down upon you and take pity. Through the blackness of your life, he will send a tiny glimmer of light, to replenish your hope and show you the way, once more.

My Life is broken
Broken beyond repair
Each day, is a day of loneliness
Loneliness and despair
I sit and at these four walls I stare
Is anybody out there?
Does anybody care?
Then, I remember... I've got...
Yorkshire tea!
Yorkshire tea!
Yessiree, that's the tea for me!
Don't need shite friends or family
No sirree, I've got
YORKSHIRE TEA!!! ☺☺☺!!!

—–

(Circa: 2013)

CAFF & JEFF

(as told by Jeff, a Cockney geezer)

My girlfriend lives next door... I call her Caff... cos her name's Caff... She works in de local caff... They call her... 'Caff of de caff'...
She come 'rarnd de uvver day for a cuppa coffee... I said... "Caff – d'you want caff or
decaff, Caff...?"
She said, "Decaff, Jeff."
I said, "Decaff, Caff..."
So, I took the lid off... an' I said... "Caff, I ain't got no decaff, Caff... You'll 'ave to 'ave caff, Caff."
So, she said, "OK, Jeff – caff."
I said, "OK, Caff – caff."
So, I took the lid off...
Den I said... "Caff... I ain't got no caff, Caff... You'll have to 'ave a teabag, Caff."
So, she said, "I'll 'ave a pyramid one, Jeff..."
An' I said, "I ain't got no pyramid ones, Caff..."
Den she said, "I'll have a square one, den..."
An' I said, "I ain't got no square ones, Caff – I only got the rarnd ones... Caff..."
So, she said, "OK, Jeff. I'll 'ave a rarnd one, den."
So, I took the lid off... den, I said, "Caff... I ain't got no rarnd ones, eever... they've run
aart..."
She said, "*Wha you on abart?* you invite me round 'ere, for a drink - then you ain't got nuffink in for us t'drink?"
Den, I said, "Caff, I got plenty in for us t'drink, Caff..."
An' she said, "Wha'...?"
An' I said, "Wo-ah (water)..."

An' she said, "*Wo-ah...?*"
"It's decaff, wo-ah, Caff."
So, she said, "Go on, den - I'll 'ave a cap of decaff wo-ah."
"Yeah – me, too, Caff," I said. "Two caps of decaff wo-ah cummin up, Caff."
So, dat's wha we done – we sat on de carch, wiv our caps of decaff wo-ah... anna box of jelly babies... watchin' our favourite programme on de telly... Mastermind.

——

(Wednesday, 5th February 2020)

CANTEEN

He looked at Charlotte. She looked at him. Their eyes met across a crowded melamine table. The smile had returned to her jaw muscles, and it was all she could do to keep it suppressed. His look became invasive, probing, almost lustful. She bit her bottom lip in a final attempt to stem the tide of titters she could feel welling up inside her stomach. She had no idea, that in doing so, she looked coquettish.

Look at the way she's biting her lip - she wants me, and she's playing hard to get.

He felt himself rising to his feet. He moved to her and grabbed her, roughly, by the arm. He dragged her to her feet - Let me go. You're hurting me. He pressed his lips against hers. She struggled to escape, but it was in vain. He clasped his hand around the back of her neck. His free hand found the front of her pink, satin blouse, and he tore it open. As the mother-of-pearl buttons bounced on the Marley tiles, he ripped the tiny bra from her pert, nubile breasts.

Gasping with lust, she succumbed - Take me, Rick - take me, now. With a sweep of his manly arm, he scattered the cutlery and crockery off the table, then threw her onto the melamine bed. As she pushed her jeans and black lace, French knickers down, over her black, lace suspender belt and black, fishnet stockings, his manshaft stood erect before her, like a meaty cucumber: thick, stiff - a full, eight inches long... no, twelve - they don't make cucumbers that small.

'Will you answer her – y'deaf bugger?' barked Dot, rousing him from his state of semi-comatose, sexual reverie.

'Wha'?'

'Have you finished with your plate?' said Charlotte, with a smile. 'Joan wants to know'.

(Circa May 2008)

An extract, from my novel 'Her Name Was Charlie', taken out during a re-write.

CAREERS ADVICE

If you want to be a critic
(But are clueless where to start)
Then listen here to this advice
Which comes straight from the heart
Don't fuster bluster, countenance
The dread that swells inside
Breathe in nice and slowly
For there's nowhere you can hide
Stop your nervous trembling
Or you'll end up in a state
Just take control, in command, and shout
"Too little, too late!"

If you want to be a celebrity
(Preferably straight from school)
You'll need a face that's built for fun
You can buy them, as a rule
The nose, the lips, the eyes, the cheeks
To stop you looking plain
Concentrate on what's on view
Don't bother with the brain
Male or female don't give up
Waste money hand over fist
If you max out all your credit cards
You might make some Z-list.

If you want to be an undertaker
(As many of us do)
Then listen here to this advice
I freely offer you

Make sure that you like corpses
Have no fear of the dead
Or you may have reached a sticking point
As you lift the old bloke's head
Stop your amateur bungling
Just do as you are bid
And try and think of puppy dogs
As your screwing down the lid.

If you want to be a footballer
(You're not the only one)
Driving round in hypercars
Earning money by the ton
While sipping on your Bollinger
You might almost forget
That plain and simple little house
You had before your jet
So, here's a thought for you, young lads
Listen, one and all
If you want to be a footballer
Learn to play football!

If you want to be a geophysicist...
There'll be some books in the library.

(Saturday, 8th September 2018)

CLASS

The working class
Are as common as grass
So many people think.
They never wash their underwear
That's why they always stink
They hang around in betting shops
Trying to win some cash
They drink a lot of alcohol
And for dinner they eat trash

The middle class
On the other hand
Are ever so polite
They've a licence for their tellies
And their washing's oh so white
And when they climb the stairs to bed
They always wear pyjamas
Their poo is such high quality
It's bought by many farmers

The upper class
I've heard it told
All die and go to Heaven
(Except the one who heard it wrong
And ended up in Devon)
They all have help, to bend the law
While feasting on their pheasant
They couldn't care about the poor
That's why they're so unpleasant

And then there's me
Now let me see
Which class do I fit in?
Working? Middle? Upper?
It puts me in a spin
I can't decide which one I am
But then I'm not alone
For we all know which class we're in
It's a class we call our own.

(Friday, 3rd January 2020)

DYING FOR CHRISTMAS

January was the best time
She always said
To buy Christmas stuff:
Christmas cards
Tinsel
Christmas crackers
Tree baubles
Cheapo presents
etc., etc.

And every year
She did the same
In January
Buying her Christmas cards
Tinsel
Christmas crackers
Tree baubles
Cheapo presents
etc, etc.
Thinking of the money she'd save

50% OFF...!
75% OFF...!
BUY TWO GET ONE FREE...!
BUY ONE GET ONE FREE...!

She'd chuckle with glee
Then lapse into a state
of reverie
Until one January

Storing her hoard in the loft
She tripped on the way down the ladder
Fell and broke her neck

And all the money she'd saved
Buying her Christmas cards
Tinsel
Christmas crackers
Tree baubles
Cheapo presents
etc, etc.

50% OFF…!
75% OFF…!
BUY TWO GET ONE FREE…!
BUY ONE GET ONE FREE…!

Went towards her funeral cost
There was no discount

Unfortunately
The undertaker wasn't one
For putting the 'fun'
Into funeral

——

(Saturday, 7th March 2020)

FAMILY LIFE

The shoes lay there for a thousand years
A million times the father had said
"Don't you think it's about time
you moved your shoes
before I trip over them
and break my neck?"
The son grunted an acknowledgement
The shoes stayed where they were

One day the father tripped over the shoes
And broke his neck
The son moved the shoes

—

This is an alligatorical poem, not to be taken gliterally.

(Wednesday, 4th March 2020)

FRANK ADVICE

Nobody lives forever
We are all sent here to die
From the day of our birth
Being placed on this earth
So, don't even bother to try

Enjoy the ride while you're here
With friends share laughter and pain
With lovers share passion and beauty
For you may never see them again

Be brave! Be bold! Be reckless!
Avoid being timid and shy
Or you won't have nowt to look back at
On that day when you're called to the sky

And if an evil tongue hurts you
Accept it with courteous grace
But if that evil tongue refuses to stop
Just rip it right out of its face

Stand up for the weak and less abled
But don't let it turn into farce
And if that big bully won't shut up his gob
Then kick him one right up the... jaxie

Be smiling, loving and caring
Even to those who you hate
For when the day dawns they all rush to your help
You'll be happy they've swallowed your bait

I know there are those among you
Who think my words fall without wit
They're mainly the ones with the serious gobs
And besides, I don't give a... toss

So these are the lessons I send to you
Laugh with me now – do not mourn
Just get behind me – form an orderly queue
'Cause the hearse driver's blowing his horn

Nobody lives forever
We are all sent here to die
From the day of our birth
Being placed on this earth
So, don't even bother to try
Amen

—

Putting the fun into my funeral

(Wednesday, 2nd May 2018)

GLASS HALF EMPTY

Just my luck
I don't believe it
The story of my life
Typical
Every time something goes right
It ends up going wrong
I've had enough
I don't want anymore
What's the point in trying?
I don't know why I bother
Well, that's it
I'm finished
Never again

I bought a lottery ticket
And won thirty million
Or so I thought
But there were two winners
I had to share it with another bloke
Now I've only got fifteen million left
Just my bleedin' luck

——

(1.10pm Saturday, 9th February 2019)

GLASS HALF FULL

At the age of 47
My mam Lizzie, died.
At the age of 54
My sister Maureen, died.
At the age of 57
My wife Sarah, died.
At the age of 59
My brother Bobby, died.
At the age of 67
My dad Bob, died.
At the age of 10
My budgie Joey, died.
That's a brilliant age for a budgie
They don't normally live that long

—

(Wednesday, 27th February 2019)

HANDY HUBBY

For his ineptitude
in the preparation
of wallpaper paste
leaving it lumpy
he was awarded
the O.B.E.

For his incompetence
In the replacing of a socket
causing the fuse box
to explode
he was awarded
the O.B.E.

For his inability
to properly secure
The wobbly garden fence,
prior to the storm
he was awarded
the O.B.E.

For his inadequacy
In fixing the bathroom leak
causing the kitchen
to be flooded
he was awarded
the O.B.E.

For all the aforementioned,
and others here unnamed,

in his persistent pursuit
of
"I'm not paying someone to do what I can do"
cheapo DIY attempts
he was awarded
the O.B.E.
by his wife:

"Oh! Bleedin' 'ell!"

—

(Saturday, 7th March 2020)

I WISH I WAS AN AMERICAN

I wish I was an American
That would be totally awesome, dude
Driving around in a twenty-foot car
Eating totally awesome food

The home of KFC and MacDonald's
Not to mention Burger King
Getting fatter by the minute
What a totally awesome thing

When sipping on my Starbuck's
And I need to go the loo
Saying "I need to use the bathroom"
Even though I want a poo

The land of opportunity
Where nothing is out of reach
Instead of a caravan in Rhyl
I'd have a condo on the beach.

And if my buddy says I'm sick
It's nothing to do with vomit
It means that we're the best of friends...
A bit like Wallace and Gromit

I wish I was an American
That would be totally awesome, bro
With my imitation suntan
And my teeth as white as snow

A chin implant! A nose job!
Even buy a sexy arse...!
On seconds thoughts... I'm British...
I don't want that life of farce!

—

(Wednesday, 19th September 2018)

IN PRAGUE:

(Scribblings done to pass the time in an hotel room, on the evening/night of Friday 28th September 2018)

I).

Friend in Need

'Don't worry if you can't work it out –
you can count on me,'
said the calculator to the pencil.

II).

The Snip

A surgeon was performing a routine vasectomy operation when he accidentally removed one of the patient's testicles. An inquiry was held, and he was asked to explain how this had happened. "I'm sorry..." he said, absent-mindedly, "I must have taken my eye off the ball."

III).

Kick the Can

My dad was born in 1909. When he was about ten, he and his mates used to play 'kick the can'. A group of them would split into two teams – one each side of the street – then, they'd throw a tin can down between them and start to play 'footie' with it, each team attempting to kick the can past the other, to score a 'goal'. They always used a tin can, which was easily purloined out of someone's bin, because in those days none of the little boys had any balls.

IV).

The Death of Ernie

(with apologies to Benny Hill)

Ernie used to be the fastest milkman, until one morning when his horse lost its grip on the ice coming down a steep hill. The cart skidded out of control and crashed, killing Ernie and smashing 200 bottles of milk. Ernie's wife came running out of the house and began screaming at the sight of her dead husband. Just then, police sergeant Pott came wobbling down the road on his bike and stopped. *"Look what's happened,"* sobbed Ernie's wife. Not noticing Ernie, crushed under the cart, the sergeant observed the scene then said, with a jaunty chuckle, to the distraught woman, *"Pull yourself together – it's no use crying over spilt milk..."*

V).

Just my Luck

Oh! How I long to find
a mate.
Am I condemned to suffer
this fate?
Two women in ten years, is not a
good rate.
How many more years will I have
to wait?
Am I over the hill? Have I left it
too late?
Blast! No chance now – this condom's out
of date

VI).

Doomed

When I turned 70, I decided to get fit and, full of enthusiasm, went to the gym for a strenuous two-hour workout, which lasted approximately eight minutes, before I stumbled out, puffing and panting. As I did, a fiddle, on the way in, jogged past exhibiting boundless energy and verve. 'Ah,' I thought, despondently, 'I wish I was as fit as a fiddle.'

VII).
P. S.
There was a naïve vegetarian who thought KFC was a football team.

If you think these are bad – they would have been worse if I'd have been sober.

(Friday 28th September 2018)

JUST MY LUCK

(Famous quotes that were **never** *said)*

“I can’t believe... that I’m one of the Beatles...”
PETE BEST.

„I can‘t believe... that my boyfriend owns Europe...“
EVA BRAUN.

“I can’t believe... that I’m the President...”
JOHN F. KENNEDY.

“I can’t believe... that Heather said ‘Yes’...”
SIR PAUL MCCARTNEY.

“I can’t believe... that this play is so good...”
ABRAHAM LINCOLN.

“I can’t believe... that I got the last seat on the plane...”
BUDDY HOLLY.

“I can’t believe... that these icebergs are so small...”
TITANIC CAPTAIN.

“I can’t believe... that no-one’s thought of this idea...”
GUY FAWKES.

“I can’t believe... that this thing flies...”
GRAF ZEPPELIN PILOT.

“I can’t believe... that these pies are selling so well...”
SWEENY TODD.

“I can’t believe... that William’s men are such poor shots...”
KING HAROLD.

———

(Circa 2017)

KEITH, THE VAMPIRE BUDGIE

One morning when Mrs Twitterby went to feed the sparrows in her back garden she found them all lying dead, on the ground. Each one had its throat torn out.

"EEK!" shrieked Mrs Twitterby, at the terrible sight.

"Never mind... you can have me, instead," said a pretty, little budgie, licking blood from its beak.

"Come in, quickly," said Mrs Twitterby, "before that horrid sparrow hawk comes back!"

Mrs Twitterby and Keith grew to love each other. Keith always looked after Mrs Twitterby, and comforted her, when things went wrong. Like the time she got up one morning and found Piddles, the kitten, with her throat torn out.

One night, as Mrs Twitterby slept upstairs, Keith sat, dozing in his cage. The window creaked open and someone shone a torch into the parlour. Two, hefty burglars, each carrying a sack, quietly climbed in.

Next morning, Mrs Twitterby came downstairs and found the two burglars lying on the carpet, each with his throat torn out.

"EEK!", shrieked Mrs Twitterby, at the terrible sight, "I must call the police!"

Mrs Twitterby doesn't live in Rose Cottage, anymore. She's doing bird, at Her Majesty's pleasure. Now, nothing gives Keith more joy than to fly through the bars each day and sit, twittering, with Mrs Twitterby... as he plans her escape.

——

(circa: 2016)

MARRIED BLISS

She picked up her case
And rushed down the hall
(the taxi had just arrived)
Then turning around
Came my peck on the cheek
As I gawped at her,
feeling deprived
'Don't forget,' she said
With a hint of concern
As she stared into my eyes...

'To take the dog to the vet on Tuesday about its diarrhoea,
The electrician's coming on Friday, six o'clock, with the solicitor's letter,
Speak to the council tomorrow about the stink from the drains
Phone the tree surgeon - urgent - about the monkey-puzzle tree
The plumber's coming, Wednesday morning, about the carbon monoxide
Pick up the parcel from the Post Office, Thursday at the latest, or they'll send it back
Don't forget your doctor's appointment about your polyps.
The fridge is full – I'll see you in a week...'

As the taxi drove off
I closed the front door
And walked down the hall with a feeling of dread
With all her words, like a washing machine
Thumping 'round and around in my head:

Take the dog to the post office on Wednesday about the monkey's

diarrhoea
Speak to the tree surgeon about the carbon monoxide, Thursday at the latest
The electrician's coming tomorrow with the doctor about the puzzle
Take the parcel to the vet on Tuesday, about the stink from the solicitor
Phone the council on Friday about the monkey's polyps or they'll send it back
Don't forget your plumber's appointment at six o'clock about the doctor's drains

I sat on the couch in a zombie-like trance
Feeling my head had been bashed by a club
Then I stood up and, putting my overcoat on,
Thought,
'Sod it - I'm off to the pub!'

—

(Thursday, 5th March 2020)

MISCARRIAGE OF JUSTICE

It wasn't me...
You've got the wrong one
Are you listening...?
I said it wasn't me
You've got the wrong one!
I didn't do it
Are you listening to me?
I shouldn't be kept in this place
I shouldn't be here
I don't deserve to be hung
What's the matter with you?
Why won't you believe me?
Can you hear what I'm saying?
Please don't hang me
I didn't do it
I didn't do it
I WAS FRAMED!

Shouted the Mona Lisa.

—

(Saturday, 7th March 2020)

OLD COWBOYS

Clint Eastwood? I remember him when
he started off – Rowdy Yates, he was, in
Rawhide.

Rowdy Yates wasn't in Rawhide. He was in
Wagon Train, with Little Joe.

Little Joe wasn't in Wagon Train, he was in
Little House on the Prairie.

No, he wasn't. Little Joe *was* in Little House
on the Prairie, but he wasn't playing *the* Little
Joe, you mean. The proper Little Joe was in
Bonanza, with Ward Bond.

Ward Bond wasn't in Bonanza. He was with
that fella with the stiff leg, who used to shout
Mister Dillon! Mister Dillon!

Chester Good.

That was him – Chester Good.

Chester Good wasn't in Bonanza – he was in
Rawhide, with James Arnaz, as the Marshal.

That was Gunsmoke

Gunsmoke was the paddle-steamer.

What paddle-steamer?

The paddle-steamer was in Maverick.

Bert Maverick.

Bert? It wasn't Bert, it was...

Bret... there was three of them –
Bret, Bart and Beau.

He used to drink sarsaparilla. He'd walk into
the saloon and say *I'll have a sarsaparilla.*

That wasn't Maverick. That was Tenderfoot.

Well, what was Tenderfoot's name?

Bodie. Someone Bodie –
sounded like an Indian.

Sioux Bodie.

Sue? That's a woman's name.

Cheyanne – that was it: Cheyanne
was in Cheyanne – not Tenderfoot.

Big fella with a shaggy fringe
hanging off his shirtsleeves.

What was his real name then?
Cheyanne Bodie?

Walker. Clint Walker.

No, it wasn't, it was Clint Eastwood.

Clint Eastwood? I remember him when
he started off – Rowdy Yates, he was, in
Rawhide.

Rowdy Yates wasn't in Rawhide. He was in
Wagon Train, with Little Joe...

—

(Tuesday, 1st October 2002)

QUACK! QUACK!

(a memory of a true story)

Having a customer, Mr Duck, coming to the showroom later in the day, to collect the car he'd bought earlier in the week, the car salesman* was at the Post Office applying for the road tax. He handed the paperwork to the lady behind the counter. She looked at the paperwork and smiled.

"It is a funny name, isn't it?" said the salesman.

"I wasn't smiling at that..." she replied. 'The customer who just walked out was called 'Mr Drake'.

—

(Monday 25th May 2020)

**I was the salesman.*

SITTING

I'm sitting here at ten past twelve
(that's ten past twelve, midnight)
I'm sitting here, forefingers poised,
And wondering what to write

I got the urge to write a poem
While in the other room
And now I've come into this one
The flower just won't bloom

I really want to write a poem
Before I go to bed
The more I think, the more I blink
My eyes are turning red

Ten minutes gone and still no poem
There must be something there
Hiding in the crevices
A thing that I can snare

Then coax it from its hiding place
And out into the light
Seventeen minutes have now passed
As onward draws the night

It's half past twelve and still no poem
My mind has turned to lead
I really wanted to write a poem...
Sod it – I'm off to bed!

—

(Started 12.10am, completed 12.39am Wednesday, 12th September 2018)

STATION ANNOUNCEMENT:

The rain now landing on platform one is for Hull, falling at: Liverpool... Manchester...

Sheffield... Leeds... and... er, would you believe – Hull. That's if it doesn't crash on the way

there. Because you can't be too careful on trains nowadays, most of the drivers are drunk.

Also, we would like to remind our beloved pains in the ars – I mean, passengers, not to leave

their bags unattended – as they'll probably get pinched, because the stations are full of

robbing bleeders who won't do a day's work – they're rather rob to pay for their drugs

because they don't get enough benefits. Then you'll only come whingeing to us, trying to

pass the buck and claim compensation, when all it boils down to is that you were too bleedin'

stupid to follow a simple instruction. Have a nice day... Which is more than I will - because

of that two-faced cow next door and her slut of a daughter, who ran off with my husband,

twenty-eight years older than her. For Christ sake, what's the world coming to when you

can't go to work with a migraine and be sent home, because you're underperforming, and find the pair of bastards in bed, banging each other like it was going out of fashion. Then he

turns 'round and says, 'you ugly bitch, I never loved you anyway – I only married you for

your money' – money which I never had to start with, I just re-morgaged my flat to make him

think I was loaded. Well that's it. I've had enough of him. I've had enough of men. In fact,

I've had enough of this shitty job and my shitty, crap life in general. So, I'm going home

now, to put my head in the oven. Do you lot hear me? I've had enough. I'm going home

Goodbye...!

I must remember to get some carrots on the way home.

—

(Tuesday, 25th September 2018)

SWALLOW TALE

How can it be?
I don't understand
How this little bird
The length of a hand
Can fly six thousand miles
Over sea and over land
From South Africa
To us, here in Britain

How can it be?
There doesn't seem a way
That this little bird
Flies *two hundred miles* a day
Feeding on the wing
It's just its done, thing
From South Africa
To us, here in Britain

How can it be?
I can't make it out
How this little bird
Will then turn about
Having raised all its young
And without any doubt
Fly all the way back
To South Africa

And then – there's me
I don't understand
The question is strangely, a big un

How I set off, at my satnav's command
And got lost, on my way to –
Wigan

—

(Thursday, 13th August 2020)

TAKE 'YORE' PICK:

There once was a young Prince Harry
Who nobody wanted to marry
'til along came a dame
Who no one could tame
Now, Harry's got too much to carry

*

A beautiful woman named Markle
To a young prince's life added sparkle
She filled him with pride
By becoming his bride
Now, his life's just a walk in the park(le)

—

(Thursday, 17th May 2018)

POSTSCRIPT:

A brash, gobby Yank named Markle
Thought Britain a quaint cash & carry
Then for all to see, she tittered with glee
As she carried off our Prince Harry

—

(Sunday, 22nd November 2020)

THE BRITISH

When it's cold we say
'Ooh, isn't it cold?'
When it's warm we say
'Ooh, isn't it warm?'
When it's foggy we say
'Ooh, isn't it foggy?'
When it's raining we say
'Ooh, isn't it wet?'
When it's hot we say
'Ooh, isn't it hot?'
When it's icy we say
'Ooh, isn't it icy?'
When it's windy we say
'Ooh, isn't it windy?'
When the weather's lovely we say
'Ooh, isn't it lovely?'
When the weather's rubbish we say
'Oh, isn't this weather rubbish?'

The British:
World Champions at
stating the bleedin' obvious

(Wednesday, 25th March 2020)

THE SMALLEST PENIS IN THE WORLD

Last night I saw
The smallest penis in the world
I couldn't believe my eyes
I looked at the thing
Then looked again
And I couldn't believe the size
The smallest penis in the world
Lying between my thighs
I quickly put my glasses on
For the third time, took a look
And the smallest penis in the world
Became a cashew nut.

—

Inspired by the seeing a cashew nut, that looked remarkably like a miniature, flaccid penis

(Thursday, 13th September 2018)

THE UNDERTAKER

(a true story)*

It was early on a Monday morning.
The car salesman was the only one
out on the site.
The garage was a large affair
dealing in car sales, exhausts,
crash repairs, tyres,
MOTs, valeting.

A black Daimler hearse
pulled onto the forecourt,
and an undertaker got out.
Looking lost,
he approached the salesman

"Hello, do you need any help?"
said the cheery salesman
to the undertaker
while thinking
I hope he hasn't come for me!

The gloomy-faced undertaker,
oblivious to his own reply,
opened his mouth and said,
"I'm looking for the body shop."
The salesman smiled

The undertaker's penny hadn't dropped
"Don't you realise what you've just said?"
said the salesman.

"Well d'you know where it is, or what?"
said the undertaker, with a growl

The salesman pointed over
to the body shop reception doors.
Twenty minutes later
the hearse drove off,
showing a huge scrape

down the other side of its body

(Saturday, 7th March 2020)

**I was the salesman.*

THE VIKING INVASION

(inspired by the poems of John Betjeman)

While driving around in our Cortinas, flashly
And pleasantly daydreaming of Laura Ashley
A quiet invasion was about to take hold
To inspire our nation to become much more bold
All caught on the hop, while we were not looking
Too busy with holiday brochures and booking
Our place in the sun, to escape from the rain
To far-distant, exotic locations like – Spain
He crept in and caught us, while we were all napping
Then, while we were packing, he was unwrapping
And when we returned to these cold windy shores
The Viking had opened the first of his stores
It was he who inspired us to chuck out our chintz
With his curtains and rugs and his oversized prints
Then furniture pieces with names that were silly
Like 'Ingo' and 'Pax' a bookcase named 'Billy'
And without realising, we'd taken his bait:
Our little twee homes looked a tad out of date
So we chucked out the chintz that we once held so dear
Jumped in the Cortina – and off to Ikea!

——

(Friday, 7th September 2018)

UP YOURS!

(a beginner's guide to becoming politically incorrect)

A whingeing Pom known as 'Limey'
Wore underpants grubby and grimy
And the stink from his feet
Smelt like rotten old meat
Cos his socks were all sweaty and slimy

An ignorant Paddy named Mick
Whose intelligence level was 'thick'
Had such a great charm
That he caused no alarm
Even though he was thick as a brick

A rough, hairy Jock named Sandy
Getting drunk on his whisky and brandy
Got a bulge in his kilt
That turned into a tilt
Then his wife said, "Och, Sandy – that's handy!"

A randy, old Taffy named Rhys
Was constantly using up grease
For the girls he'd prefer
Had no long flowing hair
Just four legs, a "baa" and a fleece

There once was a man who was French.
From his mouth came a terrible stench
Eating garlic and frog
It smelt like the bog
To his hairy-armpitted wench

An uncouth Aussie named Bruce
Had a Sheila that looked like a moose
She drank like a man
Supping can after can
Then her knickers would play fast and loose

An arrogant, dancing Kraut
Left his audience gasping with doubt
Why he had been chosen
Wearing tight lederhosen
When his frankfurter sausage popped out

So – now you know!

(Saturday, 1st February 2020)

VALENTINE
(after Carol Ann Duffy)

Not a bouquet or box of Thornton's best,
I give you: a mechanic's tool set.
It is a world, wrapped in a steel chest.
It promises gender-neutrality,
from broken nails to grazed knuckles

Here.
The last bastion of equality
will raise your anticipation,
then make your tears flow,
and stump you with frustration

I would not lie to you.
Not a cute, cuddly toy
or candlelit dinner for two.

I give you a mechanic's tool set.
Its fierce array will make you gasp:
ring spanners; open enders; screwdrivers; sockets.
A perfect set – as we are,
for as long as we both shall tolerate each other

Take it.
Its chrome-vanadium tools will let you remove
any nuts you care to.
Awesome.

And, as I cheer on The Reds at Anfield
I can relax, safe in the knowledge

that you are pleasuring yourself
on your back in the garage,
wallowing in gender-neutral delight,
like an oil and filter change
on your mother's decrepit Fiesta.

Not a bouquet or box of Thornton's best,
I give you a mechanic's tool set.
Infinitely more practical,
and ultimately less pretentious,
than something like...
an onion

—

(Saturday, 20th October 2018)

VEGETARIANS

Thank God for vegetarians
For without vegetarians
The world would be overrun
With vegetables

Leeks would stand there
Leeking all over the place
Causing the streets
To stink of leek

Bunches of Broccoli
Would form into gangs
With flick knives, wearing brockle-creepers
Like teddy boys

Spring onions
Would be springing
Into fish shops
Saying they owned the plaice

And butternut squash
Don't even think about
Butternut squash
They don't bear thinking about

Artichokes would be lurking
In the shadows
Waiting to pounce
And artily choke innocent passers-by

Runner beans would be running
All over the place
Creating havoc
Amongst the traffic

Sprouts would be sprouting up
Everywhere
Convincing everyone
It was Christmas already

Lettuce would take over
The churches
Imposing their new religion:
Lettuce Pray

Chick-peas would be
Smoothly and smarmily
Chatting up
The chicks

Kidney beans would barge
Into operating theatres
Demanding to be
Transplanted

Mushrooms would be
Telling rubbish jokes
Trying to make people laugh
Thinking they were fun guys

Beetroots would be falling in love
With everyone they met

Saying
Bee troo to me my darling

Pa snips would be
Bullying reluctant dads
Into having unwanted
Vasectomies

Thank God for vegetarians
For without vegetarians
The world would be overrun
With vegetables

—

(Friday, 6th March 2020)

WELCOME TO BRITAIN.

(a newcomer's simple guide to the complexities of British derogatory sociolinguistics)

Hello, and welcome to Britain 😊!

Lesson number 1:

How to speak in a derogatory fashion, regarding the mental capacity to absorb and assimilate information, of an acquaintance/ your boss / work colleague / neighbour / friend / member of the family / member of the general public.

Please note: these phrases must only be used in the subject's absence – not in their presence, or you might end up eating hospital food.

He/she is as thick as two short planks:

If you put a short plank on top of another short plank this would show the overall thickness – providing of course they were thick short planks and not thin ones.

He/she is a sandwich short of a picnic:

A sandwich is two slices of bread separated by a tasty filling. This name derives from the Earl of Sandwich – an enthusiastic card-player who never left the gambling table to eat, but asked his manservant to satisfy his propensity for snacking by bringing two slices of bread separated by a tasty filling.

A picnic is a British outdoor institution involving the consumption of sandwiches (see above), cakes, fruit, soft drinks, and wasps. Not to be confused with a 'Picnic' – a four-inch wafer biscuit covered in soft toffee and peanuts, coated in chocolate. Often bought as a treat for children.

He/she is as thick as pig shit:

This refers to the excrement of the porcine species. To determine the consistency of such, stand behind a pig as it starts to defecate – but don't stand too close or you might get more than you bargained for.

The light's on but there's no-one at home:

A light on in a house (at night-time, normally) usually indicates that there is someone occupying the property. Sometimes though, you will observe a light on when the property is vacant. There are two reasons for this: the light has been left on to deter burglars from breaking in, or simple forgetfulness on the part of the occupier in switching off the light.

There are, however, some people who absent-mindedly leave lights on all over the house, at all time of the day. These people are normally a sandwich short of a picnic*

* see above.

His/her lift doesn't go to the top floor:

This refers to high-rise buildings (e.g. blocks of flats) that contain a lift for the purpose of elevating people, and goods, to the top floor. A lift that only went to the penultimate floor would not be of much use for those wishing to go all the way to the top, as they would have to get out and walk up the final flight of stairs. This could be a problem if they were disabled, obese, or disabled and obese. Conversely, they may be in the position of, for example, having to carry a coffin down from the top floor.

*If you are an American reading this, it will be clearer if you substitute the words lift, floor, and flats with the words: elevator, level, and apartments.

If dynamite was brains, he/she wouldn't have enough to blow his/her hat off:

Dynamite is an explosive made of nitro-glycerine, sorbents, such as powdered shells or clay, and stabilizers. It was invented by the Swedish chemist and engineer Alfred Nobel* in Geesthacht and patented in 1867.

The saying refers to the miniscule amount of dynamite that would be required to blow someone's hat off. Obviously, the dynamite would need to be ignited to achieve this end, otherwise it would be harmless. It is actually a misnomer because, it doesn't have to be a hat but could be any other type of head covering e.g. a cap, a scarf, a fez, a sombrero etc. A more accurate way to describe it would be 'If dynamite was brains, he/she wouldn't have enough to blow his/her item of head apparel off.'

*not to be confused with the term 'no bell'. Used, for example, in the sentence 'This bicycle has no bell.'

So there. I hope I've cleared up your confusion regarding the complexities of British derogatory sociolinguistics and you'll be pleased to know that you can to look forward to **Lesson number 2**, in which we'll explore the origins and explanations of simple, well-used, British terms such as 'clear as mud'.
So, until next time, toodle-pip, old bean, here's mud in your eye!

(Saturday, 14th March 2020)

ZIGG, FROM THE PLANET ZOGG

Many moons ago, the evil Zoggians decided to set up a breeding station on earth, the purpose of which would be to, eventually, take over the planet. Commander Dark 111 and Corporal Zigg were sent to establish this station, the commander remaining in the mothership, as Zigg was sent down to begin the mission.

Early that evening, so as not to give the game away, Zigg transformed himself into a human image and was waiting on the pavement. As a woman approached, he started to say his carefully rehearsed chat-up lines...

"Greetings, female... you will be pleased to know that the sight of your overlarge mammary glands fills me with delight... I will now lead you to a feeding establishment, where you will recline and consume many edibles articles, as I fill you with intoxicating liquids, the purpose of which, you will be happy to know, will be to get you inebriated.

Having achieved this, I will then lead you to my abode, where we will ascend to the sleeping quarters, strip naked, and lie on the sleeping platform. I shall then impregnate you will my breeding liquid. You will be delighted to know that within six weeks you will be the mother of my Zoggian sprog."

Unfortunately, the mission never got off the ground. After many failed attempts that evening, Zigg was commanded back to the mothership to explain why.

"Did you repeat, exactly, word for word, the script that I wrote for you?" shouted the angry commander.

"Yes, sir..." said Zigg.

"Did you remember to say that you had a penile appendage that could achieve a length of twelve earth-inches when fully extended...?"

"Oh..." said Zigg, sheepishly. "I am sorry, commander, I

forgot that bit."

Commander Dark 111 flew into a rage.

"Get back down there and start again! And don't forget about your penile appendage!"

After many more attempts, the mission was abandoned. Back on the planet Zogg, Commander Dark 111 was awarded a medal for his bravery in piloting the mothership through the universe. Zigg was demoted, from corporal to private, for his incompetence. He was sent into exile and spent the rest of eternity hoovering the moon.

(Wednesday, 20th November 2019)

Love

1st ANNIVERSARY

(to my wife, Sarah)

To the world, you are one person
But, to one person - you are the world

I love you x

(29th July 1989)

A BUCKETFUL OF DAFFODILS

Three weeks since the meeting of eyes
two weeks since the pressing of lips
now hand in hand
a cold Sunday in March
they make their way to the landing stage

He stands at the entrance
with a bucketful of daffodils:
rough-looking Scouser in
a rough-looking overcoat
'Daffs 20p a bunch'

Their fingers separate as she
carries on walking obliviously
down the gangway
he gives the bloke 50p
lifts two bunches out the bucket

Water dripping from sodden stems
he rushes to catch her up
takes her finger-tips and turns her
she smiles seeing the sleeping flowers

'Will you marry me...?'
nothing in response
except her mouthful of laughter
and the sinking of his heart

As Overchurch heads out into the Mersey
the Liver Building shrinks before their eyes

sixteen months later a shower of confetti
twenty-two months later their baby is born

(Wednesday, 11th March 2020)

A THOUSAND MILES

I lie here thinking of you: a thousand miles away, but I can see you clearly. Lying in your
bed, snuggled up, fast asleep, softly breathing into your pillow. As I lie here looking at a
cratered white moon, pasted to the sky, surrounded by a scattering of diamonds. I want you
but you are a thousand miles away. A thousand miles. A thousand miles from me.

My love for you is an open wound which will not heal. A constant ache reminding me that
you are a thousand miles away. We share the same cratered white moon but are divided by a
thousand miles of earth. You came late into my life because of circumstances I had never
foreseen but coming late into my life you became the light of my life across a thousand miles.

I lie here thinking of you. I close my eyes to see your smile. I hear your laughter. I feel your
breath upon my cheek. I feel your warmth against my body. I need you but you are not here.
You are a thousand miles away. I open my eyes and see the cratered white moon slowly
being shrouded by a veil of grey cloud. Our moon. Our cratered white moon now gone.

Disappeared. As I think of you a thousand miles away. Lying in your bed, snuggled up, fast

asleep, softly breathing into your pillow. Lost in dreams. Until tomorrow. When you will

remain the same as tonight; a thousand miles away. The veil of grey cloud drifts from the

face of our cratered white moon. I turn and close my eyes as I send to you my love across

a thousand miles.

—

(Tuesday, 10th March 2020)

AUNTY NORA

She kept her love
Locked up in a box
Never sharing it
With anyone
Never allowing it
To be free
To see
The light of day

When she died
They buried her
With her love still locked
Inside the box
For she had never
Set it free
Never met the one
Who, held the key

—

(Wednesday, 4th March 2020)

Written in memory of my beloved Aunty Nora, my mam's sister, she was a second mother to me. Although she loved her niece and nephews with all her heart, she never found anyone to share her own life with.

CARELESS HEART

(a sonnet)

Now, listen well; beware, my careless heart
Lest you be touched and captured, once again
By eyes that shine and tender lips that start
The bittersweet cascade of love's refrain
For, in your senseless, tripping, headlong rush,
Angelic choirs descending from above,
With breath, a barely restrained, trembling hush.
Beware the fall – the one that ends in love
Take heed these words, my foolish, careless heart
Lest you be touched, and captured, once again
For tender lips that kisses will impart
Can leave behind a yearning, lost-love pain
And so, this new-found, warming, summer breeze
May lead the way into a winter freeze

—

(Monday, 14th December 2020)

FIRST LOVE

Where are you now, I wonder. I am here,
Still me, thinking of you. After a lifetime of life
I am still here, thinking of you: the ABC Minors,
The Secret Seven, the Famous Five - and you -

Sitting beside me in Miss Brennan's junior class
Me: the rag-arsed scallywag from Mill Lane
And you: The Princess Royal from Queens Drive
With a telly, hot water, a garden, and food

I wonder what became of you. Did you suffer the
Slings and arrows of outrageous fortune, or did you
Just stay single. Maybe become a nun, or a doctor,
Solicitor, work for the Crown Prosecution Service

Or settle for the till in Tesco. And now – ten times older
Than when I first fell for you, looking back on a life of
Laughter and tears, happiness and heartbreak, I wonder
what might have happened if by some freak of nature, we

grew up and spent the rest of our lives together, had kids,
bought a house – maybe even a Rubik's Cube. Would we
still be together now or would death have us parted (again).
I don't know. I'll never know, so I'll rewind back to 1955

To the days of Sunday Night at the London Palladium, the Adventures
of Robin Hood, Double your Money, the Knockout, the Beezer, Bob Hope
and Bing Crosby, Dean Martin and Jerry Lewis, Choc-Stix,

Bubblies, penny
Arrow bars, Roy Rogers, the Lone Ranger and Tonto, the Cisco kid and Poncho,

And leave it, there x

—

(Wednesday, 11th March 2020)

FOR SARAH
(SHE IS HERE)

I will not speak in solemn words
For she was not the solemn one
Nor will I think with thoughts of dread
For she is here, although she's gone

I see the laughter of her smile
I hear the echo of her voice
For with each thought she reappears
And she is here although she's gone

Yes, she is here inside my heart
Residing in a special place
And in the mirror of my soul
I see reflections of her face.

How can I speak in solemn words
While wildflowers nod and skylarks sing
How could I think with thoughts of dread
As grey clouds part her sun to bring

Yes, she is here with every breeze
Within each raindrop, every leaf
And when the snowflakes start to fall
I'll feel her kiss upon my cheek

———

(7th April 2009)

Written for my wife, Sarah, 1952-2009, the day after she died.

FOR YOU

(sonnet #2)

For you, how long will my love still remain?
'til all the leaves of autumn stay on trees
'til crashing waves no longer show disdain
'til all the morning songbirds fail to please.
For me, how long will your love still enthral?
'til all the bells of life will chime no more
'til all the rains of Heaven cease to fall
'til pipers disappear from ev'ry shore.
For you, how long will my love still remain?
'til snows of winter fail to disappear
'til moorland winds no longer do complain
'til springtime swallows fail to reappear
For you have made my heart an open door
For you, my love will last forevermore.

—

(Friday, 18th December 2020)

FOREVER, YOURS

(For Maria)

There is a place within my heart
That only you and I can share
A special place that brings me joy
For I know that you're always there
Far from the bitter tears of life,
And there, I know you'll always be
A special place within my heart,
A place reserved for you and me

Far from the heartbreak left behind,
We two can share a happy day
Beyond the sorrow and the grief,
For there, I know you'll always stay
There is a place within my heart,
That all the years will not replace
I close my eyes, and journey there
Then, once again, I see your face

My little one, who went before
Your eyes could open on this world
Please do not fret, there is no cause
For mummy's here,
Forever, yours.

(Saturday, 5th September 2020)

FRIEND

(about mental health and looking after each other)

When all your birds have flown away
When all your clouds have turned to grey
If all you seek is another day
I will be there for you

When all you need is someone kind
When troubles gather in your mind
If you are feeling left behind
I will be there for you

When fate deals you a losing hand
When no-one else can understand
If life seems like a foreign land
I will be there for you

If in the future, you behold
Life's really, not that pot of gold
When you just need a hand to hold
I will be there for you

—

(Saturday, 11th July 2020)

GRANDCHILD

To my grandchild, who I will never see
I will never hear your laughter
I will never wipe your tears
I will never hold your hand
We will never walk together
Past lakes and streams
Or through a sun-dappled wood
We will never share the beauty
Of a blackbird's song
I will never see you grow
And take your first, faltering steps
I will never read you a story
And tuck you in at bedtime
Then watch you drift away
Into your private land of sleep
Yet, in spite of all these things
Through time and space
Always remember
With every step you take
That I will be beside you
And always hold dearly in your heart
These words which I send today
I Love You

(Thursday, 11th May 2017)

L.O.V.E.

Lost in a forest of your smiles
Out on a limb, terrified to look down
Valid reasons not to fall in love
Enshrined in the thrill of desire

Long ago our eager eyes met
Over the years we drifted apart
Valentine cards: no longer sent
Enrapture: a thing of the past

——

(Monday, 9th March 2020)

LOVE POEM
(IT DOESN'T WORK THAT WAY)

My heart says

'No
Don't go, just yet
Please
Stay a moment longer...'

I need to wrap my arms around her
feel the warmth of her body
next to mine
surrender to her embrace
feel our hearts
exchanging beats
to place my cheek against hers
and close my eyes

a moment...
a moment...

then, look upon her face
and now we have to say 'goodnight'
But I don't want to...
I want to stay with her
To be with her
Where she goes, I want to follow
To curl around her
As we drift into sleep
But no,
It doesn't work that way

And as I press my mouth to hers
I close my eyes again
And taste her tender lips
Upon mine
Then as we part
she smiles and says
'Goodnight...'
I return her smile and say
'Goodnight - see you in the morning...'

And when she turns
I watch her leave the room
I want to stay with her
To be with her
Where she goes, I want to follow
To curl around her
As we drift into sleep
But no...

It doesn't work that way

——

(Thursday 9th April 2020)

MARY & PADDY

(inspired by the true story of my Grandmother and Grandad)

1961:

Eyelids beneath pennies, holding them shut
Face now at rest on her silver hair,
As a kid sat and watched from a hand-me-down chair,
On her living room bed, amid hushed, Catholic prayer
Ganny Owens, at peace, no more burden for her

The day before, her clinging to life
My Ganny Owens, a dutiful wife,
Had opened her eyes, from the edge of death
Raising her hand, to the foot of the bed
"Alright, Owens, I'm coming now..."
Her words whispered out
As Grandad's soul waited, to guide her away
Just as he'd done on that long ago day,
Back to his Roscommon roots

Circa 1900:

In his search for work, from the Emerald Isle,
He'd journeyed across the Irish Sea
Young Paddy Owens, an Elphin lad,
Stepped off the ferry, at the Liverpool quay
Lost and alone, in the great unknown
Eighteen years old - a Navvy, to be

How could he have known that she'd be the one?
How could she have known that he'd be the one?
As he travelled the miles from the Pier Head
To the rough-ready district known as Old Swan

To there, lose his heart to a fifteen year old scouse
Daughter to those of a lodging house
Where young Paddy Owens arrived there to glean
The sparkle and warmth from his new-found colleen

Mary and Paddy, so the story began
For the young English girl, and the young Irish man
With a signature forged, the document said
That Mary was sixteen, and so, she could wed
Then back on the ferry the newlyweds went
To the Emerald Isle, no more need for consent

So, the years passed by, and Mary became
As Irish as shamrock, her heart was aflame
With everything Irish: 'Ireland's Own', snuff,
Leprechauns, banshees, she couldn't get enough
But not just in folklore were 'little people' known
For Mary and Paddy had a brood of their own…

After to-ing and fro-ing to Ireland and back
They settled in Old Swan with young baby, Jack
Then came another, another and more
You needed a pencil to keep up the score!
For handsome young Paddy and his beautiful wife
Produced life, upon life, upon life, upon life

Sixteen, in total:
Rose and Anne (twins), Agnes and Jane (twins), Bridget and Timmy,
Mary and Nora, Paddy and Jack, Nellie and Martin, must have kept hands busy
Oh, and of course, there's another, I forgot, Elizabeth, my mam,

known also as 'Lizzie'.

But this record now takes a poignant turn, and doesn't end happily, the way that it should
For many of these little ones, my aunties and uncles, didn't manage to reach the end of
childhood.
Plus, a third set of twins, prematurely born, and a stillborn baby, for hearts to mourn.

1954:
In 18 Mill Lane, sat a young scouse lad
Looking down the back yard as his Irish grandad
Came shuffling up, Sunday morning, each week
His thunder now gone, he was humble and meek
With his flat cap, muffler, and simply clad
For his weekly shave, performed by my dad

But a lifetime's hard work had now taken its toll
And strong, young Paddy was now weak and old
Plagued by ill health and burdened with age
My dear grandad's story had reached its last page
As the colt, *Never Say Die* won the Derby, that day,
Paddy Owens closed his eyes and drifted away

Circa 1956:
Off he goes, down the Swan, a little scouse kid known as 'Franny'
Hand in hand, on their way to the shops, the little scouse kid and his ganny
Though money was scarce, she'd root through her purse, and find there, a few spare coppers
Or maybe Joey, a Tanner or a Bob, What a pair of extravagant

shoppers!
Then coming from Reece's with a big bag of 'brokes', young Franny would skip like a flea
What more could you want? Broken biscuits galore and a big pot of ganny's sweet tea!

1961:
Eyelids beneath pennies, holding them shut
Face now at rest on her silver hair,
As I sat and watched from a hand-me-down chair,
On her living room bed, amid hushed, Catholic prayer
Ganny Owens, at peace, no more burden for her
For now, she had stepped through that final door
And Mary and Paddy were reunited once more

—

(completed 26th December 2020)

The salient facts of the above poem are, to the best of my knowledge and belief, true.

They have been handed down to me by my Aunty Nora, and from my Aunty Nora via my niece, Elizabeth Roberts.

The day before Mary died, my Aunty Nora and Uncle Martin (her daughter and son) were sitting in the room, where my ganny, propped up on pillows, lay in bed. There had been no sign of life for a long time. Then, she opened her eyes and looked toward the bottom of the bed. She raised her hand and said, "Alright, Owens, I'm coming now..."

Nora and Martin looked toward the bottom of the bed. There was nobody there.

The day after, my ganny died.

MY SLEEPING BEAUTY

I stand beside you and watch you
as you sleep
gently sleep
If I leant down
and pressed my lips to yours
would you be released from your spell?
like the sleeping beauty
Would your eyes open
Those eyes
that lit the fire in me
all those years ago
all those years ago
It seems like yesterday
Would your mouth spread
into its child-like smile
once again
I hardly dare to breathe
in case you wake
as I gaze down
at your face
That beautiful face
The face that saved me
Now resting
sleeping
At peace
At peace with the world
as I stand and watch you
sleeping
Gently sleeping
In your coffin

—

(1st March 2020)

The final farewell to my wife, Sarah, April 2009.

SHINING STAR

There is a star
That shines brightly
Through the black
Of night
Shining down
Shining down

Through the clouds
Of heaven
Through the dark
Of mind
Into my heart
Into my soul
Always
And forever
Shining down
Shining down

Into the mirror
Of my past
Reflecting memories
Toward the vast beyond
Of future times
Of yet to be
Shining down
Shining down

Steering
Guiding
Calling me

One day
When I am free
Free
From the bonds of life
To venture forth
And be
Within the glow
Of that shining star
Shining down
Shining down

When
A kaleidoscope of dreams
And laughter
Envelopes me
No more alone, will that star be
For we will shine

Together

——

(Tuesday, 17th April 2018)

Written in memory of my mother, Elizabeth Jones, 1912-1959. She died of a heart attack at the age of forty-seven. I was eleven years old at the time.

SUPERHERO

Superheroes don't fly through the sky,
stop speeding bullets,
shoot spider webs from their wrists,
because they don't exist.
They are fantasy characters,
the creation of fantasy minds.
But I once knew a superhero
of flesh and blood,
of muscle and brawn.
He worked the land, during the war.
driving his tractor,
doing his bit, year after year,
putting food on people's tables,
filling British bellies,
to beat the Fuhrer.
And, when peace reigned once more
he moved onto a different land,
a land of fumes and noise,
of sweat and flames and heat,
doing his bit, year after year,
after year, after year,
putting food on the table,
and a roof over the heads
of his wife and family.
And now,
his final move,
at the age of ninety-seven,
to be with his beloved Mary.
Reunited forever.
A man of flesh and blood,

of muscle and brawn.
A cheeky man, of pride
guts, integrity, and laughter.
A man of steel.
My second father.
A superhero.
His name was George.

(24th April 2020)

A tribute to 'the dad I never had', George Hirons, who passed from this life on the 23rd April - St George's Day. He was a victim of Covid 19.

SWEET DREAMS

I long to lie between your thighs
And kiss you gently on the lips
As we make sweet and tender love
And from this sweet and tender love
Our hearts will fill with wild desire
And write a symphony of passion

And afterwards as we lie
Within the peace that only love can find
I will kiss you gently on your sleepy eyes
And we will drift away, into the land of sleep
Where together, we will share
Sweet dreams.

—

(Circa: 2013)

THANK YOU

You bring a song to my heart
You are the music of my soul
You are the sunshine in my mind
You bring beauty to my thoughts
You are the warmth of my chill
You are the laughter in my life
You brought the breeze that dried my tears

Thank you

—

(Friday, 30th June 2017)

Written for my dear friend, Svatava 'Beruska' Psurukasova.

THE THIEF

How can I look upon your beauty?
How can I gaze into your eyes?
Feel that touch of your tender breath
Upon my cheek like a warm sunrise

Share the joy of your innocent laughter
Comfort you when you shed your tears
Feel the delicate kiss of your lips
Soothing away my anxious fears

How can I breathe your intoxicating fragrance?
Cocooned in the silk of your feminine art
Without surrendering all that I am
Without you stealing my heart

—

(Monday, 9th March 2020)

TOO SOON

Not for us, to grow old together
Sharing the twilight years of our lives
With you in a wheelchair, me with a limp
Like so many other husbands and wives

No, not for us the thrill of the chase
Just ambling along to the end our days
Bickering over which stair lift to choose
Or discussing, in depth, our incontinent ways

At the end of each day, when tired and limp
On the couch with each other, both accepting our lots
With a saucer of Hobnobs and a small pot of tea
Comparing the sizes of our liver spots

While counting the pennies we haven't got left
No browsing around in mobility shops
Enthralled by the merits of raised toilet seats
'Til my swollen prostate, the conversation stops

At hospitals, dentists, ophthalmic opticians
No endless appointments that we have to keep
About asthma, arthritis, and other conditions
About eyeballs and earholes, flu jabs, and teeth

'That telly's too loud. Turn it down!'
        'I can't hear it.'
'Where's you hearing aid?'
        'I can't remember where I left it.'
'What did you take it out for?'

'The battery went flat.'
'Well, put another one in.'
'I don't know where I've put them.'

No... not for us to grow old together
Holding onto the glow of our fading moon
It's the hand we were dealt by the man in the sky
Even though, I know, you were taken too soon

I love you

(Saturday, 11th April 2020)

TRUE LOVE

You are the one that I would choose
To give all my Maltesers
I'd even pluck your bushy bits
So delicately, with tweezers
And if you were feeling peckish
You could have half of my Snickers
I'd even wait in Primark's queue
To surprise you with new knickers
Yes, I'll be there without a care
For a cuppa and a chit-chat
To give you a smile once, in a while
And two fingers of my Kit Kat
And when you're feeling down and out
When the world won't seem to budge
I'll come running to the rescue
You can finish off my Fudge
And when your ointment has run out
And you're scratching on your scabies
Who gives a care? We'll just sit there
Biting heads off jelly babies
Yes, I'm the one, to rely on
When your life has hit a dip
I'll let you lick the fondant
From inside my Walnut Whip
If it's adventure that you seek
And you're looking for some kicks
I'll take you down to Aldi
To buy those phoney Twix

So, there you have it.

What else more
Can I say or do?
Except to use these little words...
I
Love
You
Xxx

(Wednesday, 16th December 2020)

VICTORIA SPONGE

(Katie's Tea Rooms, Chester)

Who would have thought,
That such simple things
Could provide the sparkle
I've seen in your eyes,
The delight on your face
At things commonplace
Like toasted crumpets
Stilton cheese
And of course
Your Cornish ice cream

Again, the sparkle in your eyes
The delight on your face
As we sit down
In our favourite place.
Though, hot crumpets and Stilton
Served up in a trice
Are all very nice
They cannot compare
To your favourite fayre:
A slice of Victoria sponge

Our clash of cultures
Isn't a clash
It's just you and me:
A meeting of minds
A blending of hearts
Two wandering souls
No longer apart

Now sharing their happiness
With a pot of green tea
Between you and me

And a slice of
Victoria sponge

Miluji tě
xxx

—

(Tuesday, 3rd March 2020)

YOU

I think of you
When the moon sleeps
Like a ball of gold
Upon a painted sky

I think of you
When tears of rain
Fall from the clouds
As the darkened heavens cry

I think of you
When whispering winds
Sweep through the branches
Of lazily swaying trees

I think of you
When snowflakes fall
And icy fingers form
When streams and rivers freeze

I think of you
When sunbeams dance
With sparkling glee
On the surface of a lake

But most of all
I think of you
With yearning soul
And heart and mind
Each moment that I wake

—

(Circa: 2013)

Miscellaneous

ANOTHER YEAR

Snowdrops break free from their crystallized glistening tombs
Banshee winds wail
In frozen fields lambs make their first pathetic bleats
Cock Robins fight
On slender twigs buds are swelling, preparing to burst into life
Sleeping soil wakes
The wailing wind loses its voice: *in like a lion, out like a lamb*
Frogspawn appears
Lonely single swallow arrives here, sits on a telegraph wire and wonders...
Where are the rest?
Sun smiles down on waving fields of golden wheat, barley and maize
The jealous rain cries
Ladybird climbing up a poppy stem opens its wing cases and takes flight
A rainbow appears
Many sweeping swooping swallows now, across the fields and farmyards
Hedgehog babies feeding
Red Admiral, wings apart, soaks up warming rays then lays its eggs on nettles
A skylark sings
Busy bumbling bumble bees move from bloom to bloom on sweet-smelling lavender
Apples fall to earth
Trees change colour preparing to surrender their dying leaves to the gusty wind
Swallows gather on wires
Beneath dappled oaks, acorns crack underfoot as schoolboys

play conkers
Bats are serenading
Plump ripe blackberries overflow the spiny tangled mass of hedgerows
The rowan radiates
Swans and geese arrive from frozen northern lands to Britain's warmer climes
Ivy is flowering
The trees have gone to sleep – the swallows gone. The wind cools
Hedgehogs hibernating
The air is as pointed and sharp as glassy broken icicles
Breath tumbles from mouths
Mother Nature dressed in her filigree finery of frost
Landing ducks' slide
Ivy-clad trees reach up their dead naked branches to the frozen sky
Dormice are snoozing
Cold black cemetery stone reads 'Laurence Parsons'
My beloved friend
Another year come and gone devoid of your laughter
'Merry Christmas, Mister Laurence'

——

(Friday, 14th September 2018)

ASHES

Spring at Coniston
Her ashes scattered upon
They sink, then are gone
Forever

—

(2018)

CHESTER
(DEVA VICTRIX)

Millions of people over two thousand years
Have climbed these steps that I climb now.
Millions of people over two thousand years
Heard this river gurgle as I hear it now

Millions of people over two thousand years
Have walked past these stones that I walk past now
Millions of people over two thousand years
Have circled these walls that I circle now

Leaving behind indelible scars
Like their fingerprints
As will ours

From the Romans, to the Saxons,
From the Vikings to the Welsh
From the Normans to the Stuarts
To the Tudors
The Georgians,
The Victorians,
The Edwardians

All with their laughter
All with their tears,
All with their banter
Their intoxicating fears
Plodding along in an endless rhyme
To all disappear down the passage of time
As will we.

Leaving Chester to stand
Unbroken.

(Friday 28th February 2020)

CRAP LIVES MATTER

In an underpass
Through the cider's haze
The broken souls
Spend their broken days
As people walk past
With their eyebrows raised
"It's their own fault,
They should learn
To mend their ways"
The streets of Britain
Are paved with gold
And so, she believed
Every lie she was told
By the evil tongues,
Who then trafficked, and sold
Her into a life of Hell
He sleeps in a box
On a city's street
An invisible man
To the passing feet
Through the winter's chill
And the summer's heat
He sleeps in a box
On a city's street
Pummelled until
she was black and blue
with all she stood up in
to the night she flew
seeking refuge from carers
she now sleeps alone

away from the fists
and beatings

—

(30th September 2020)

GAWJUSS

I
am
GAWJUSS

I know Im GAWJUSS cos Im constantly
told this by my hundreds of friends on facebook
every time I upload a selfie they post comments like

Babe, you are GAWJUSS...
U look amazin...
Wit woo sexy wench...
Check u out just gawjuss as usual xxx...
U so pretty I wanna put you in my lunchbox...
Sooo BEAUTIFAAAUL.

Of course Im GAWJUSS dont need
them to tell me

my extensions are GAWJUSS
my eyebrows are GAWJUSS
my eyelashes are GAWJUSS
my tan is GAWJUSS
my teeth are GAWJUSS
my nails are GAWJUSS
my sexy pout is GAWJUSS

U dont spend this much
money without lookin
sooooo sexy an
GAWJUSS

(Thursday, 12th March 2020)

Inspired by juvenile, sycophantic Facebook jargon.

GHOST OWL

As dusk settles down on the tangled field
With the sun sinking low to the eye
From her secretive place she gently steals

Launching herself to the evening air
A velvet phantom on translucent wings
Silently gliding her task to prepare

Scanning below with her moon-like face
Through brambles, tussocks and weeds
Gliding and flicking and gliding with grace

Her sudden screech then shatters the still
And a vole below freezes with fear
Like a stone she plummets down for the kill

She spreads her wings and again takes flight
To return to and nourish her young
Then back on her beat 'til the end of the night:

The ghost owl

—

(Tuesday, 23rd March 2020)

GRAVEYARD

(on passing Mickle Trafford graveyard, on Christmas day, 2019)

Where have they gone
Who bade farewell to their used-up lives,
The ones who laughed and cried and fussed
Who left behind their bones and dust,
Beneath forgotten soil

Whose hearts once filled with Christmas joy
With song and fear with love and dreams
The ones who spun a thousand tales
Who walked a hundred twisting trails,
Beneath an endless sky

Where are they now
Those who have ventured further on
Have they now reached their journey's end?
Their final story now been penned
For where they've gone, we follow

—

(Wednesday, 25th December 2019)

IF THE CAP FITS

With your two-faced smiles
And your crocodile tears
You strung me along
For all of those years
You had me believe
That you were my friend
But now I've seen through you
This is the end

With your working-class cap
And rolling your own
And your red-topped rag
Who could have known
Deep down you were Tory
Buying your council house
And queue-jumping doctors
For your poorly spouse

In church Sunday mornings
With the rest of the pack
Red wine and wafers
Patting each other's backs
So Catholic and humble
Arse-licking the jerks
So sad you've forgotten
How true friendship works

You hated the one
Who I loved the most
Yet you came to her funeral

Was that just to gloat?
She spoke with an accent
That you chose to fob
It's called double standards
You inverted snob

So, gather them round you
The poor and the lame
Spread your coins wisely
To embellish your name
Saint Terence of Runcorn
Take them all for a ride
Until they discover
That you've nothing inside

(Circa: 2013)

INVISIBLE TEARS

I am a woman
Why do you treat me as a man?
I am a woman
Can you not see me as I am?

All my life I have walked in your shoes
Closely imitating your masculine ways
Never discovered the courage to choose
Groping my way through a manly haze

Existed in your shadow
Lived my life in the dark
Hiding behind a man's façade
Been too afraid to imprint my mark

Now that I am a woman
Why do you still see a man?
Now that I am a woman
No longer one of your clan

All my life since an innocent boy
I have been too afraid to reveal my tears
Never have I felt interminable joy
Nobody there to allay my fears

Existing in confinement
Living life in a mask
Hiding behind your bravado
Been too afraid to differ, to ask

All my life I have walked in your shoes
Closely imitating your masculine ways
Never discovered the courage to choose
Groping my way through a manly haze

And now that I am a woman
Why do you still see a man?
Yes, I now am a woman
Why can't see me - as I am?
?

—

(Tuesday, 17th March 2020)

JESS

She was quite partial to a glass of whisky, was Denice. Normally, it was just the one glass

with ice, but not tonight. She'd drunk three quarters of the bottle. Glenfiddich. Her favourite.

When it was a present, of course. She couldn't normally afford to buy malt whisky herself.

Unless she dropped lucky on a scratch card or something. Maybe a Christmas or birthday

present from someone. She knocked back the dregs of the glass and decided that she was

going to do it, tonight. Now. Yes. What had been tumbling around in her mind for the last

twelve months was going to be given its wings tonight. Set free to fly. As the last mouthful

found its way down her gullet, she made up her mind. There was no point, you see. No, no

point in carrying on. She could no longer bear the crushing weight of the grief and loneliness

that smothered her heart, her soul, her existence. One amount of grief could have been

bearable, but two? in such close succession? To lose the two people that she loved most in all

the world. She placed the glass onto the coffee table, stood, walked into the hall, took her coat off the banister and put it on. She walked out the front door, leaving it open, and made

her way down the path. She noticed how beautiful the sky looked; a large, silver moon

surrounded by dozens of stars, standing guard. What a perfect night to die, she thought.

Would they both be waiting for her, up in Heaven, she wondered. Mind you, would she go to

Heaven, after committing suicide. Not according to her religion. Fuck her religion. What had

her religion ever done for her, apart from heap guilt upon guilt, onto her fragile mind and

scrounge money on the plate. She made her way across the field opposite, climbed over the

fence, then half-slid down the embankment, until she reached the hard shoulder. She stood,

wavering slightly. She turned her head to the right and looked at the various vehicles

speeding toward her, most in the middle lane. She needed one in the first lane. Big, heavy,

thundering. A lorry. No good fucking about with a pair of pensioners in a Micra, on their way

home from the bridge club. No. They'd probably die of a heart attack before she did, when they saw her jump in front of the car. No. It had to be something big, heavy, thundering. She

was pissed but not pissed enough to realise that she wanted to be killed outright. Not stuck in

some bastard intensive care unit for a few weeks, with tubes and monitors all over her like

they were going out of fashion. Poor nurses. As if they didn't have enough to contend with,

without some looney tunes who'd tried to kill herself. All this, and with a rumbling stomach

at two o'clock in the morning, thinking 'why the fuck did I want to be a nurse?' With that in

mind, she decided to make a proper job of it. She looked up the motorway. Nothing, except

cars in the middle lane. Then in the distance, through the moonlight, she could see a huge pair

of headlights, six feet apart, with coloured lights, like a mini, Blackpool illuminations. Yes, it

was a lorry, bearing down fast. All she had to do was just wait until it was twenty foot away

then walk into its path, then it would be over. All gone. Bye-bye. Goodnight. Closer and

closer the lorry sped. She inched her way to the edge of the hard shoulder. Closer and closer, the lorry approached. Her eyes overflowed with tears as she silently said goodbye to her mum

and dad, begging their forgiveness. From a hundred yards the lorry's air horns blasted, as the

driver saw how close she was standing to the road. She prepared to take her final step, in this

life. She closed her eyes. And then, as she prepared to step forward... a whimper. She

became distracted from her mission, her goal, by a whimper. The whimper grew louder. She

turned. Somewhere in the overgrown tangle of long grass and weeds came a whimper, a

gentle cry for help. Her eyes scanned the rough grass as the whimper grew louder. The lorry

sped past, the draught from the giant almost blowing her off her feet. She ventured forward

into the grass, guided by the whimpering. And there she lay, a young border collie x springer.

A reject. The sort of dog that everyone pretends to like but nobody wants. Its tail began to

wag as Denice looked down upon the pathetic bundle of black and white fur, dumped from

her heartless owner's car, only to be hit by another as she ran, confused, around the motorway. 'Hello, sweetheart,' mumbled Denice, as the dog whimpered louder, the pain

from its broken leg tempering its feeling of happiness. She reached down, and, as her fingers

began to stroke the dog's ear, a soft, warm tongue licked her wrist. Through her alcoholic

haze, she realised she wasn't the only one who had problems of despair. She carefully lifted

the dog and, through yelps of pain, cradled it in her arms. She stumbled back up the

embankment, over the fence then across the field, toward her opened front door. She lay the

dog onto her bed, covered her with a blanket then lay down beside her, stroking her head

and comforting her. They became inseparable. They'd saved each other's life, Denice and

Jess.

——

(Sunday, 22nd March 2020)

KING DAVID

I was born into, and brought up in, the lap of luxury, think; silver spoon, sailing on the lake,
childhood motoring holidays on the continent, boarding school education, never wanting for
anything. I am the product of a red brick university and am one of the professionals. I know
the right wines to drink, the right books to read, the difference between U and non-U. I take

walking holidays in the Alps, drive a prestige car. I am cultured. I look down upon people
beneath me, obviously, because they are beneath me. Factory workers, bus drivers, council
dogsbodies, etcetera, etcetera: the working class. Common people in their matchbox terraced
houses. Common people leading humdrum, ordinary lives. I deal with them every day in my

professional life. The thought that the like of them can cross-fertilize with the females of our
class, produce half-breeds, abhors me. They should never aspire to climb out of the gutter. To
live above their station. What we have is ours, and only ours, not to be shared with the like of
them. Leave the vintage port and stilton to us. Stick to your keg beer and pork scratchings...

BASTARDS.

(Monday, 16th March 2020)

LAURENCE

(a eulogy for my dear friend, Laurence Parsons)

Since the 1st of May, the day Lol was called to that 'Big Car Boot Sale in the sky,' I've come to feel that a day without Laurence Parsons is like a bacon butty without sauce... a cup of tea without milk... a pint of bitter without a head on it... The days are still the same, but there's something missing. There's a void which can't be filled.

I knew Lol longer than I knew my wife. They're probably up there now, the pair of them, having a whinge about me. I can just imagine what he'll be saying to her "he'd mither a nest of rats..." But that was Lol - the tough nut with the soft centre. The one who kept his guard up, until you'd proved yourself to be deserving of his loyalty, then that was it – you couldn't wish for a better fiend – sorry, I mean friend!

And when he introduced me to Damian, the three of us gelled immediately. We became the three handsome, rugged, dashing, young blades about town – well, that's what we thought, anyway – but really, we were just Cleggy, Compo and Foggy.

And now the three are just two... Because he's gone... I can see him now, wandering around that 'Big Car Boot Sale in the sky,' looking for Isle of Man souvenirs for Jeanne. And then he'll be off – into the charity shops. Looking for even more trinkets to display proudly in his beloved 'Parsons Arms' – Well, Lol - I'll drink to that. Bottoms up!

Laurence: 1948-2016, Rest in Peace.

LIVERPOOL

Liverpool, my Liverpool
So silently you lie
Beside the Mersey, deep and cool
And watch the ships go by
Whenever I am far away
And feeling so forlorn
My thoughts return to Liverpool
The place where I was born

I have walked your broken streets
And darkened alleyways
I have crawled your gutters
When my mind was in a haze
And still you cast your spell on me
With the feelings you impart
You're still the one who holds the key
To the gateway of my heart

And ever since a little child
So many years ago
When smiles, then tears, then laughter
Became my ebb and floe
Each time life tried to knock me down
With your blood in my veins
When all those tears had disappeared
Your laughter, still remained

Liverpool, my Liverpool
So silently you lie
Beside the Mersey, deep and cool

And watch the ships go by
And now that I am far away
And feeling so forlorn
My thoughts return to Liverpool
The place where I was born

—

PIGS

It's not within my nature
to follow 'Pig at the Trough' politics,
where the one who pushes the hardest
gets the most food.

Apart from anything else, I think it degrading.
I wonder if the expedients of this behaviour
have ever wondered how they are viewed
through the eyes of others.
Probably not.
It's not within their nature.

Someone once said,
'What does it profit a man if he gains the whole world
yet suffers the loss of his soul?'
I agree.

(10.18am Tuesday, 22nd January 2019)

HAIKU
(5-7-5)

Spring at Coniston
her ashes scattered upon.
They sink, then are gone

Summer sun smiles down
on waving fields of wheat.
The jealous clouds cry

Surrendered leaves fly
in the wild gales of autumn.
The trees go to sleep

Winter cold stone reads
the name of Laurence Parsons:
my beloved friend

My love I send you,
like tiny falling raindrops.
Landing on your heart

Large snowflakes falling
past the lamp like drunken moths.
A white carpet forms

Peacock, wings apart,
soaks up the warming sunshine.
I blink and it's flown

For You...

I cast my eyes out
across the angry ocean.
The wild wind curses

Tiny ladybird
climbing up a poppy stem -
spreads its wings then flies

My love I send you,
like stars to light up the dark.
And guide me to you

Hungry cock blackbird
tugging hard, on stubborn worm.
Poor worm! It snapped!

Single swallow here
alone on telegraph wire.
Where are all the rest?

Sweat peppers my brow
fingers black from Mother Earth.
I smell a teapot.

Beneath dappled oaks
acorns cracking underfoot.
A pheasant's loud croak.

My love I send you,
like a million poppy seeds.
To grow in your heart

Clouds black with anger
as they bathe in gold sunshine.
A rainbow appears.

Confessional box
I kneel and confess my sins.
The priest softly farts.

Fog drifting slowly
wrong way down a one-way street.
Nobody complained.

I peel off her clothes...
She stands before me: naked
I feast – banana!

On my darkened path
He crunches beneath my sole
Goodbye my dear snail

—

(ongoing)

REUNITED

The mighty steam engine slowly hissed and rumbled its way into the station, the carriages creaking, brakes quietly squealing, as they followed their mistress along the track. Under the smoke-stained canopy, gradually slowing down, the Princess Elizabeth locomotive reached walking pace, then a crawl. He picked up his suitcase and leaned out of the carriage window to search for her, along the platform. As his left hand rested on the door handle, his breathing quickened in anticipation. With a slight jerk the train came to a halt as it gently nudged the buffers. In the distance, through a mist of vapour, stood a dark-haired woman of forty-seven.

It was her.

Standing.

Waiting to see him once more.

As her eyes searched the length of the carriages, a single door opened and an old man, carrying a suitcase, precariously, carefully, eased his way down the step and onto the platform.

It was him.

He turned to face her.

After a lifetime of waiting, all that separated them now, the only barrier left that stood

between them, was a walk of fifty yards. He put his case down onto the platform. He no

longer needed the detritus of a bygone life that it contained. His journey that began at the age

of eleven, had finally reached the end he had, for so many years, wished for. Too nervous to

smile, he began to walk toward her. Slowly at first, then he felt his pace quicken, as his eyes

began to make out those never-forgotten features: the brunette hair; the high cheekbones;

the thin lips - which were now separating into her smile.

Closer and closer.

His emotions became a jumble of contradiction.

Should he laugh?

Should he cry?

Should he shriek with joy?

As he approached her, his faltering steps slowed to a halt. She was there – after so many

years – standing three feet in front of him. His eyes began to well with tears and his mouth

began to tremble. She placed her fingers onto his lips...

"Shhh... It's over... you're here, now... that's all that matters."

He wrapped his arms around her and began to sob.

As she hugged him in return, his sobbing destroyed her

composure. She pressed her cheek

against his and they shared the bitter tears of love. Then, as their eyes met, a mutual smile

graced their lips and she kissed his cheek. She took him by the hand and their fingers

entwined. They turned and left the platform as the train, and the station, slowly evaporated,

until they had disappeared.

They carried on walking, hand in hand, a mother and her son:

so cruelly separated in life,

now reunited forever,

in death.

—

(Saturday, 15th July 2017)

When I am reunited with my mam, I'll be older than her.

SMALL TALK

ME

I always tried
to be the dad
like the one I wanted
but never had.

—

(10.24am Tuesday, 22nd January 2019)

LIMERICK

There was a young lady from Chester
Who loved eating fruit picked in Leicester
Whilst eating a plum
She swallowed her mum
And it took seven weeks to digest her.

—

(2015)

A VOCAL EXPRESSION EMITTED, INSPIRED BY THE INITIAL IMPRESSION UPON FIRST SETTING FOOT INTO THE CAVERNOUS NAVE OF THE ANGLICAN CATHEDRAL, ST. JAMES' MOUNT, LIVERPOOL.

Wow! isn't it big?

—

(Saturday, 21st March 2020

ANY EXCUSE

I was going to wash my windows
But a mouse was asleep in the bucket
Plus the fact that my chammy was stiff
So I gave up thinking, oh - never mind.

—

(Sunday, 5th January 2020)

CRACKERS

Fried eggs aren't all they're cracked up to be… or not to be, that is the question

That isn't a question, it's a statement.

What is?

Fried eggs aren't all they're cracked up to be.

I know – I just said that. Weren't you listening?

—

(Friday, 14th September 2018)

THE DECREPIT OLD NON-PC WIDOWED PENSIONER BLOKE WHO STILL HASN'T GIVEN UP ON THE FAIRER SEX

Maybe if I became
A lesbian
I'd have more chance
Of pulling
The birds

—

(Tuesday, 10th March 2020)

FALLEN ANGEL

"Small scratch..."
The needle goes in...
The blood is extracted...
The nurse softly farts

—

(2019)

ODE TO DIARRHOEA

Man's best friend is the bog!

—

(Tuesday, 16th June 2020)

BINMEN

We are the disgruntled binmen
Embittered by our enslavement
So, we throw half the rubbish into the truck
And the other half onto the pavement

—

(Saturday, 20th June 2020)

Inspired by the amount of rubbish I pick up, after the binmen have left the scene of the crime.

GOLDEN ANNIVERSARY

Damian's road was long and hilly
Until the day that he met Gilly
Then, his life was turned to laughter
And they both lived 'naggilly' ever after.

—

(Thursday, 9th January 2020)

With love to my two, dear friends Damian and Gilly on the occasion of their 50th wedding anniversary (which, incidentally, coincides with my 72nd birthday, but the less said about that the better ☹!!).

SOME MEMORIES FROM MY CHILDHOOD

Telly adverts:
You'll wonder where the yellow went
when you brush your teeth with Pepsodent,

Coates comes up from Somerset
where the cider apples grow,

You'll look a little lovelier each day
with fabulous cream of Camay,

There was a young girl from South Bend
who had only *throppence* to spend
But what could be nicer
than a Pendleton's Twicer
ice cream with a lolly each end

OMO washes not only clean
not only white – *but bright!*
OMO adds bright bright brightness.

The Flicks:
Lash LaRue, Hopalong Cassidy, George Formby,
Jayne Mansfield, Sabrina, Diana Dors, Doris Day,
The Three Stooges, Bud Abbott and Lou Costello,
Flash Gordon, Norman Wisdom, Old Mother Riley,
Tom & Jerry, Heckle & Jeckle, Mighty Mouse,
Bugs Bunny, Woody Woodpecker, Popeye,

Music:
Frank Sinatra, Frankie Vaughan, Dean Martin, Elvis,
Bill Haley, Connie Francis, Fats Domino, Anne Shelton,
Lonnie Donegan, Shirley Bassey, Liberace, Perry Como,
Ella Fitzgerald, Jerry Lee Lewis, Little Richard, Mantovani,
Ruby Murray, Lita Roza Mario Lanza, Sammy Davis Junior

My mam:
'No, Bob – please don't hit me again.'

——

(Thursday, 12th March 2020)

SPARROWHAWK

Feathered javelin
with eyes of a devil
skimming the gardens
up
down
up
down
over the hedges
over the fences
up
down
up
down

A flight of death
to the prey in its path
unaware
oblivious
to the rollercoaster
approaching
up
down
up
down

then panic!

An explosion of fear
terror-stricken
the flock scatter,

except one
now gone

Snatched

in the talons
of the javelin of death
with the eyes of a devil

Sparrowhawk

—

(Monday, 23rd March 2020)

THE ANIMAL

Tentative fingers of morning light
Dispelling lingering threads of mist
Eerily crept through the slumbering trees
Wherein, on a carpet of soft pine,
It lay
No longer imprisoned within the womb
Encouraged by its mother's nose
It rose
Shakily, on wobbly legs
To its feet
As months passed by,
It grew
Into a masterpiece of nature's hand
It lived
It roamed
Born Free, Living Free, Forever Free
Until the day
The animal arrived
Then, shot from a blast
Of the animal's gun,
It fell to the ground
Its lifetime done
All for the sake of someone's fun
It died

—

(Friday, 5th May 2018)

THE BEAUTY OF MODERN ART

In my opinion
the beauty of some modern art
is that it requires neither beauty nor art
to achieve its status

For example
it doesn't need the hypnotic atmosphere of a Turner
or the visual heartbreak of a Van Gogh
or the naturalistic captivation of a Vermeer

For example
I could buy a ten-foot square canvas
get myself down to B&Q and buy a load of various cheapo paints
throw the said cheapo paints all over the said ten-foot square canvas
roll around naked on it
ride my bike over it
walk over it in ever-decreasing circles wearing my hiking boots

Then
splatter it with globules of diarrhoea

Then
give it a pretentious enigmatic title such as 'My life #3'

Then
sign it something like 'Jason Bollock'

Then
out of the total population of the world

a miniscule minority (which would still be a sizable number)
would hail it as a masterpiece

even though it's literally just a load of shit

but that's the beauty of some modern art
it requires neither beauty nor art
to achieve its status
(it's the same with poetry, such as this)

Mister Turner, Mister Van Gogh, Mister Vermeer et al…
Why did you bother?

—

(Tuesday, 1st October 2019

THE COCKY WATCHMAN

Back in the fifties' when I was a lad
Building sites always had:
A Cocky Watchman

An old bloke, who came on at dusk
And sat until dawn
In front of his brazier
Giving a yawn:
The Cocky Watchman

Sitting there all night, on his Jack Todd
Warming his nuts and praying to God
That nobody came on the site
On the rob:
The Cocky Watchman

The last line of defence
Against vandals and thieves
Was this dozing old bloke
Who no-one believed,
Could do anything:
The Cocky Watchman

But things were different
Back in those days
Even vandals and thieves
Had respect for old age:
The Cocky Watchman
Then dawn would break
And the sun would rise

So, he'd gather his things
And head home to his wife:
The Cocky Watchman

He'd climb into bed
And go out like a light
Sleeping all day until it was night
Then back he would go
To fight the good fight:
The Cocky Watchman

(Friday, 6th March 2020)

THE INVISIBLE ONES

Who can they turn to?
When all the doors are closed
(happy husbands, happy wives,
busy people, busy lives)
How can *they* comprehend,
From their chocolate boxes
The feelings
Of loneliness
Isolation
And despair
That dwell within a soul.
When all the backs are turned
When all those who loved
And were loved
Have now gone.
And all that remains
Are the drops of a life
Yet to be poured
But remain ignored
Remain ignored
Who can they turn to?
Who?

—

(Sunday 14th April 2019)

THROUGH A CHILD'S EYES

My dad
Cooks my meals
They're shite
His peas are like bullets
His spuds are like cobbles
His beefburgers make the smoke alarm mental
It's shite

My dad
Washes and irons my clothes
They're shite
My shirts are scorched
My trousers are creased
My underpants have turned pink
It's shite

My dad
Tells me jokes
They're shite
Not even funny
I don't understand them
But I pretend to laugh
It's shite

My dad
Cries a lot, of a night
It's shite
He thinks I don't know
But I hear him, in his room
As he whispers and cries

It's shite
He keeps asking God
Why he took my mam
It's shite
She's not here anymore
She's not coming back
Get over it, dad, even though

It's shite

(Circa: 2013)

UNSUNG HERO

She came into the showroom
An elderly woman
I stood and smiled
She needed a smaller car
She gazed at my desk – her mind in disarray
Her son made an excuse for him and me to stand
As she sipped her coffee, her son and I sauntered outside
He asked that I forgive his mum's present state
She was still grieving
Grieving the death of her husband

He'd been a pilot in the Polish Air Force
When the Nazis conquered Poland
He fled to Britain and joined the RAF
As a fighter pilot
He flew a Spitfire
Fighting in the Battle of Britain
Becoming one of 'The Few'

When peace returned
He made Britain his home
they met
Fell in love
Raised a family
They reached old age
Together
Loving their garden
Planting
Tending
Pruning

One day
Feeding a bonfire
He accidentally tripped
And burnt to death
Before her eyes

What the Nazis had failed to achieve
His garden had accomplished

(Monday 2nd March 2020)

The Pandemic

CAPTAIN TOM

He never walked alone
For every step of the way
Captain Tom was not on his own
For day, after day, after day
This hundred-year-old British lion
Through determination and grit
Shone a light into the darkness
And was followed by every true Brit
Showing the world, the breed that we are
Here, in our British Isles
That no matter how tough the going gets
We can still fill the world with smiles
So, there you have it
Captain Sir Tom
Let us all give credit, where due
When the going got tough - you got going
Captain Tom, we all salute you.

—

(Tuesday, 2nd February 2021)

CORONA: EASTER DAY 2020

Here's my advice to Corona
You despicable, life-taking loner
Don't think you will beat us
You'll never defeat us
'cause this time next year
We'll still be here
Plodding along
With a joke and a song
And where you've been binned,
no mystery:
Consigned to the sewer of history
With leprosy, polio, smallpox
We'll just shut you up in a box
'cause the vaccine is coming to get you
To eradicate you and destroy you
You won't get away
That's the price you will pay
Running out is your time
You won't break our front line
Of scientists, doctors, nurses, and carers,
Of police, soldiers, shop staff, drivers,
and workers,
When our back is against the wall
That is the time that you will fall
That is the price that you will pay
For taking innocent lives away
And now your time is running out
Now it's your turn to feel the clout
'cause the vaccine is coming to get you...

(written Easter Sunday morning, 12th April 2020)

ONE DAY, SOON

One day, soon
Our sun will shine again.
One day, soon
Our clouds will drift away.
One day, soon
Our thoughts will still the pain.
One day, soon
We'll find another way.
One day, soon
No more, this sad refrain.
One day soon
No more will we delay.
One day, soon
Our strength will break this chain.
One day soon
Our debt no more to pay.
One day, soon
Our eyes will smile again.
One day, soon
Our hearts will seize the day.

One day, soon…
I promise.

——

(Sunday, 24th January 2021)

SMILING EYES

Will he ever see the faces
belonging to the eyes
that smile above the Covid masks?
"Name and date of birth...?"
she asks in a gentle voice.
"The same as yesterday," he quips,
attempting to be witty, while trying to ignore
he's in his socks and without his trousers.
Having given the details
he climbs onto the bed.
Warm hands gently manoeuvre him
into the exact position
as pleasantries are exchanged.
Then it becomes serious:
they concur with each other
as they concentrate on the screen.
Their dedicated professionalism
coming into sharp focus,
as he becomes a target for the beams.
The warning buzzer sounds.
"OK, Frank, be right back...."
Jess Glynne stands in a crowded room
as he lies alone.
The Varian eerily hovers then moves into various positions
above its prey.
He stares at the two faces in the clouds,
as the invisible beams are fired.
Five minutes later,
"All done..." she says, cheerily, as she returns.
He climbs off the bed,

no longer noticing he's in his socks and without his trousers
"See you tomorrow," accompanies the smiling eyes.
He thanks her and leaves the room.

Will he ever see the faces
belonging to the eyes
that smile, above the Covid masks?
The eyes of Rachel
And Rachel,
Of Jasmine
And Kirsty,
Of Clodagh
And Lowri,
And, of course,
Scouser Ritchie.

The answer is no.

But I don't need to see your faces
to recognise the kind of heart
that beats within you all...

Thank you.

—

(5th August 2020)

THE CHARGE OF THE FRIGHT BRIGADE!

(after Alfred, Lord Tennyson)

Half a yard, half a yard,
Half a yard onward
Straight through the Aldi doors
Charged the six hundred
'Forward, the Fright Brigade!
Charge for the shelves!' he said
Straight through the Aldi doors
Barged the six hundred.

'Forward the Fright Brigade!'
Panic-stricken and dismayed
Idiots without a clue
As they plundered
Theirs not to make reply
Theirs not to reason why
Theirs just to *BUY! BUY! BUY!*
Right through the Lidl doors
Crashed the six hundred

Bog rolls to the right of them
Pasta to the left of them
Crowded aisles in front of them
Pushing and shoving
Pensioners can go to Hell
Boldly they snatched as well
Soup, beans, sanitizer gel
Charging through Morrisons doors
Panicked the six hundred

Flashed all their banknotes bare
Flashed as they turned to swear
Wheelchairs *'Get out of here!'*
Barging an army while
Those with sense wondered
Plunging with push and poke
Straight for the tills to choke
Sainsbury's gone up in smoke
Pillaged and plundered
Smashing through Tesco's doors
The nutcase six hundred

Coffee to the left of them
Tea bags to the right of them
Bare shelves behind them
Volleyed and thundered
Storming in panic's swell
Onward! they must not dwell
They that have crushed so well
Selfish and greedy – *sod off the needy!*
While conscience and manners fell
Trampled the six hundred

When will their panic fade?
O the wild charge they made!
All the world wondered
Dishonourable, the charge they made
Dishonourable, the Fright Brigade
Ignoble six hundred

—

(Thursday, 19th March 2020)

THE FRONT LINE

(for Adele)

Do your best
To wipe us out
Bring us to our knees
Fill our hearts with tears
But you will not succeed
We did not choose this job
This job chose us
And here we stand
Together
An impregnable,
Unbreakable wall
A wall of defiance
Determination
Dish it out
And we will dish it back
A hundredfold
We fight
We fall
But we rise
Again
And again
For you will not break us
A dam of defiance
In the face of death
We will conquer
You will not win
You will not beat us
You will not succeed
For we are here

The front line
Not just for today
Because when you are a memory
Consigned to the gutter of time
We will still remain
A wall of defiance
Determination

Unbroken

—

(Tuesday, 13th January 2021)

War

BLITZ

Hitler, Adolf Hitler,
You psychopathic god
Do your best to break us
But it won't be good enough
Send your Luftwaffe over
Raining bombs galore
For our island fortress must be crushed
Or you have lost the war

Try your best to break us
Bring us to our knees
Drive us underneath the ground
Destroy this Bulldog Breed
Do your best to break us
Make the going tough
Try your best to break our hearts and souls
But it won't be near enough

'Cause we'll all pull together
Oh, we'll all pull together
Yes, we'll all pull together
In this tug of war
Oh, we'll all pull together
Yes, we'll all pull together
Like we've just never done before

Though the world is dark and lonely
Our beacon still shines bright
But we fear that we're the only ones
To put paid to the march of the Reich

So, we'll all pull together
Oh, we'll all pull together
Like we've just never done before...

'My old uncle 'enry had a pair of pearly gates
Twenty foot wide, five higher
'Til one day he got a letter, taking them away
Now they're in the wings of a Spitfire! '

'Cause we all pull together
Oh, we all pull together
Like we've just never done before
'My mother put in front of me
A meal what looked so meek -
One egg, one slice of bacon
I thought 'what a bloomin' cheek! '
And when I pulled my mother up
Her voice began to peak
'MEAL? That ain't no meal...'
My darlin' mater daintily murmured
'THAT'S TO LAST YOU ALL THIS WEEK!'

'Cause we all pull together
Oh, we all pull together
Yes, we all pull together
In this tug of war
Oh, we'll all pull together
Yes, we'll all pull together
Like we've just never done before
Though the world is dark and lonely
Can we see a distant light

Does the wild Atlantic's awesome roar
Conceal a fearsome bite
America...
America...
America...

—

(Written in 1983)

CHRISTMAS DAY 1914

Amid the rats and the shelling and blood
The power of evil gave way to the good
As the guns fell asleep
With their hate buried deep
Tommy and Fritz kicked a ball in the mud.

—

(Saturday, 25th December 2004)

CITY OF DEATH
(HIROSHIMA)

Fortunate were they who were incinerated by the blast: not for them the horror that

followed. In a second; thousands, from a being to a shadow of ash - vapourised, gone.

Not for them to witness the City of Death, for they were taken first, to go where the rest

would follow. Not for them to see the walking corpses, dressed in their shrouds of peeling

skin, their charred and bleeding bodies, their lidless eyes, their half-faces gaping: the living

dead. Walking over countless remains of swollen-bellied bodies, guts boiled within by the

heat. Aimlessly walking north south east west hypnotised by the shock of horror. And into

the river to find solace from their screaming burns, the human lemmings leapt by the

thousand until they formed a solid mass, drowning those who lay beneath. Not for them

to hear Kazu shouting her mother from beneath the rubble, *'Mummy, mummy, pull me out.*

The fire is coming. Pull me out.' Not for them to hear the breaking of a mother's heart as

her daughter burned to death. Fortunate were they who were incinerated by the blast. Not for them to hear the cries of '*Water... water...*' from the roasted multitude and see the

sky open and black rain falling. Not for them to see them cup their hands and hold tin cans

and drink the radioactive ash-stained water, then suffer a lingering death from radiation.

Not for them to see the final death count reach a hundred and thirty-five thousand.

Fortunate were they who were incinerated by the blast in the City of Death.

—

(Sunday, 14th October 2018)

A 'city of death' was the description given by an 18 years-old female office worker, when she stepped out from her office, after the blast. She'd survived because she was lucky enough to be in the basement of the earthquake-proof office block.

D-DAY

They came
Out of the sea
Crashing ashore
Wave after wave
A tide of humanity
Unstoppable
Determined
Into wave after wave
Of bombs and bullets
Tearing through flesh
Destroying young lives
From a sea red with blood
Across bloodstained sands
They charged
Wave after wave
Determined
Never to give in
Never to fail
For the sake of mankind
To destroy the evil within
They saw the job in hand
Across the sand
Of hedgehogs, barbed wire, a million mines
Rommel's wall
Destined to fall...

They dropped
Out of the sky
By the thousand
A torrent of courage

A storm of humanity
Unstoppable
Determined
Into a sea of fire
Across blood-drenched fields
They charged
Wave after wave
Determined
Never to give in
Never to fail
For the sake of mankind
To drive the evil within
Back to the gates of Berlin
They saw the job to be done
The prize to be won
The wrong to be undone
They conquered

—

(8th June 2018)

REST IN PEACE

Beneath the soil
In foreign fields
At rest, the young men lie
Caressed by the wind
Blessed by the sun
Forever, to face the sky

How long, will we appreciate
The sacrifice they gave
In handing us our freedom
As they marched to an early grave?

Young lads, young men
All as one
Of laughter and of tears
Of broken hearts
Of beer and darts
All wrapped in tender years
Of football, sweethearts, motorbikes
The innocence of the young
Torn from their grasp
By the wail of death
No more, their song to be sung

How long, will we remember them
And the sacrifice they made
In granting us our future
It can never be repaid

Beneath gravestones

Far from their homes
In death, the young men lie
Row, upon row,
Upon row,
Upon row.
Forever, to face the sky.

―――

(Sunday, 29th October 2017)

I consider 'Rest In Peace' to be the best poem that I have written. I doubt I will ever write another poem to compare with this one. Here is how it came about...

REST IN PEACE - evolution

I wrote the war poem 'Rest In Peace' over a period of one and a half hours on the evening of Sunday, 29th October 2017.

Although I'd written poetry, on and off, over the previous fifty years, the thought of writing a poem to the war dead had never crossed my mind. With hindsight, I think the idea might have been lying dormant within my subconscious, waiting to emerge.

The reason I say this can be traced back to the summer of 1994. My wife and I had taken the children on holiday to France. Having twice visited Brittany in previous years, we decided to visit Normandy, for a change and, also, to tie this in with the 50th Anniversary of D-Day.

While in Normandy, without the children, we visited one of the war cemeteries. It was a devastating and humbling experience. As far as the eye could see, row upon row, upon row, of young men's gravestones stretched into the distance, in a sea of white.

For quite a while I walked between the graves, reading the inscriptions. The majority, of the men, were aged between 19-25. It was a deeply moving experience.

On the weekend that I wrote the poem, I had a friend from the Czech Republic staying. Her name is Beruska (my wife died in 2009). On the Saturday, while sightseeing in Liverpool, I took her into the bombed church of St Luke's and our conversation turned to the war. Later in the day, she asked me what, was the significance of the poppies, being worn by people. I told her about Armistice Day and the Festival of Remembrance, at the Royal Albert Hall. I mentioned the sea of young men's graves that I'd seen years earlier, and she was greatly saddened.

Having dropped Beruska at Manchester airport on the Sunday afternoon, while driving home, I switched on the car radio. The beautiful 'Benedictus', by Welsh composer Karl Jenkins, was playing. It is one of the most beautiful, and haunting, pieces of music I've ever heard. Throughout the journey home, the words 'gave' and 'grave' kept coming into my mind.

I arrived home, had something to eat, and put the telly on, to settle down for the evening with a bottle of beer and a film. But I couldn't settle. I kept thinking of the words 'gave' and 'grave' and Karl Jenkins' beautiful melody wouldn't leave me. I turned the telly off, found a pen and piece of paper, and sat on the couch. I put the pen and paper onto the coffee table, and as I began to think of those countless young men who'd never returned home, the words 'beneath the soil,' and 'far from home,' came into my mind. And so, I began to write the poem.

Frank – Friday, 3rd November 2017.

NIGHTMARE

From the depth of humanity
I pray unto you, dear God
Wake me from this nightmare
For such monstrous deeds cannot be real
Each day I witness horrors
The like of which I cannot comprehend
From the depth of depravity
I beg of you, dear Lord
Wake me from this evil
Open my eyes
And take away the visions
That paralyse my soul
Take away the screams of the innocents
The gaping stares of the walking dead
The sickly-sweet stench of the crematoria
The acrid black curling remains of your children
That search their way to Heaven
If this is not a dream, then my time is near
My Final Solution has arrived
From the depth of my soul, dear Lord
I cry unto thee
I cry unto thee
I cry unto thee
Father in Heaven
Hear my voice
And wake me

—

(7.45am Thursday, 7th February 2019)

OVER THE TOP

(inspired by the poetry of Wilfred Owen)

We crouched like diseased tramps, racked with pain.
Young Tom, crying in fear.
Harry, vomiting violently into the mud.
Some mumbling through half-forgotten prayers, as if there was a God.
Others stared like corpses, with premonitions of the ugliness to come.
The only ones who had any semblance of sense, among that Hell of madness, were the rats,
who scurried from scrap to scrap, oblivious to the fate of their superior beings.

'Ready lads!' He shouted, as if we were going on a jolly jaunt.
Seconds later, the whistles blew.
Up the ladders we surged.
Out of the trench.
Over the top.

Roaring with false bravado, we charged
toward the roaring, relentless clatter of the guns.
They began dropping around me. Young Tom copped it first.
I made it one hundred yards before I was hit.
One took off my left ear, another burst through my jugular,
the third straight through my ribs and into the top of my lung.
The force sent me spinning into a shell crater.
I landed on my front and managed to roll over, before losing consciousness.
And there, in that crater, my life came to an end as I choked
on vomit and blood.

I was twenty-two.
For me, it was over.
For thousands more, until the Armistice, it was about to begin.

—

(Sunday, 23rd September 2018)

PALS

They were not soldiers, those who went
Happily, off to war
Pals together toward their deaths
From the horror that lay in store
Of slaughter from the starving guns
None of this foreseen
By the *'Pals Battalions'* from the cobbled streets
To the glorious fields of green

They were the volunteer army
'Lord Kitchener Wants You'
The poster said patriotically
As the clarion bugles blew
And so, the call was answered
By the thousands signing up
To taste the Devil's banquet
And sip from the poisoned cup

The fresh, the young, the gullible
All swallowed Rawlinson's ruse
Convinced that they were soldiers
And eager to pay their dues
Friends and colleagues' side by side
Through the flaming gates of Hell
As the generals played their heartless games
The friends and colleagues' fell
They were not soldiers, those who went
Marching to the Somme
The Marne or Ypres or Amiens
Just Britain's naive sons

Busmen, binmen, labourers
Dying shoulder to shoulder
You can put a uniform on a man
But it doesn't make him a soldier

(Tuesday, 30th October 2018)

"I remember when the news came through to Accrington that the Pals had been wiped out. I don't think there was a street in Accrington and district that didn't have their blinds drawn, and the bell at Christ Church tolled all day."
Percy Holmes, the brother of one of the Pals, remembers what happened when the soldiers from Accrington didn't return home.

RUTH

She was the last of the morning's arrivals. Naked, she entered from the disrobing

room. Twenty years old. Beautiful. She walked toward the stool. In his eyes there

was no lust. In her mind no embarrassment. Out of humanity, he gave her the semblance

of a smile. She sat, well-aware of the fate awaiting her. Her eyes displayed neither fear

nor agony of any kind, only boundless sadness. With both hands he gently stroked

her long silken hair toward the back of her head, then gathered it into a ponytail with

his left hand. He picked up the clippers and began gently working from the front of

her scalp toward the rear, trying not to snag them. 'What is your name?' he asked.

'Ruth,' she replied. 'Ruth Dorfman.' As he continued, she told him she had recently

finished college. Then, she asked quietly, 'How long will I have to suffer?' He paused,

momentarily. 'Only a few minutes,' he replied, knowing it would be more than thirty.

Tears welled in his eyes as he finished shearing her hair. She stood and gave a long, last look, as if saying goodbye to him and to a cruel, merciless world. 'Thank you,' she

said, quietly, then walked slowly and calmly toward the chamber. 'SCNELL!' the guard

shouted, as he pushed her inside, then slammed the door shut and bolted it. A few minutes

later the tank engine roared into life, pumping in the exhaust fumes.

(Tuesday, 2nd October 2018)

Based on a true occurrence, that took place at Treblinka death camp, Poland, 19th January 1943.

THE BATTLE OF BRITAIN

In 1940 when Hitler's greed
Had terrorised Europe at breathtaking speed
Into each country the Nazi had pushed
Poland had fallen, resistance was crushed
France lay in ruins, Scandinavia raped
Wherever the eagle flew nobody escaped

When Britain refused the Fuhrer's demands
And held out alone against Hitler's commands
The fate of our nation nobody could tell
Nobody could see such a blistering Hell
Would become the result of his temper's eruption
He put Britain next on the list of destruction

He called his chief marshals to draw up a plan
Of how he could quickly take over our land
The date was set, the invasion was nearing
The honour was given to Air Reichsmarshall Goering
To demolish our airfields in the path of a blitz
From Dorniers, Heinkels and Messerschmitts
With our air force in ruins our defence would be lost
The eagle would drop on its prey unopposed
After the Luftwaffe would come the invasion
For Goering had promised yet on this occasion
He had not reckoned on Dowding's young men
Or the devastating punch of Mitchell's gem

On the tenth of July, the raids began
Coming over the Channel the radar could scan
A large cloud approaching our Southern shores:

Enemy aircraft arriving in scores
Their deep-throated droning had captured the air
All Britain stood silent, united in prayer

For the impatient young pilots, the order was "Scramble!"
The fighters took off on their greatest gamble
For to win this battle every trick must be used
But they could not win - yet dare not lose
Into the heavens they raced one by one
To surprise their attackers from out of the sun

Spitfires, Hurricanes - any plane that flew
All went up for the nation knew
That should we fail now in our darkest hour
The Hun would be waiting, ready to devour
Our towns and our cities - all would be smitten
And rubble would lie where once stood Great Britain

Twisting and turning, machine guns loud
Bringing death and destruction from out of each cloud
Rapidly climbing then into a dive
A swarm of angry bees protecting their hive
"Red leader, to green. Red leader, to green...
Bandit on you tail. Bandit on your tail..."
Fighting and dying, no spirit to lull
Like terriers snapping at the heels of a bull

But just when we thought we had driven them back
They'd return twice as strong in fiercer attack
Wave after wave casting shadows of death
As young pilots burned the world held its breath
Hopelessly outnumbered by five to one

The magnificent "Few" bravely fought on

Clawing at devils became our plight
Screaming defiance became our delight
Three thousand Swastika-clad aircraft
The might of the Fatherland's Luftwaffe
Where murdering our loved ones and destroying our homes
On our island of freedom, the dice had been thrown.

—

"Never, in the field of human conflict, was so much owed, by so many, to so few..."

Winston Churchill. August 20th, 1940.

(Written circa: 1970. Revised 2017)

THE LITTLE SHIPS
(DUNKIRK)

Trapped like rats in a barrel, cut off by the sea
A third of a million souls in the jaws of Hell
Strafed, bombed, blasted
On the barren dunes, their hope deserting them
Replaced by death and destruction
Unleashed from Stukas, Messerschmitts
Never again, to look upon the faces of their loved ones, friends

As the end drew near
*'Where is the fu***** RAF?'*
And, as they cursed, the Spitfires and Hurricanes
Invisible, inland
Held back the might of the Fatherland:
Baying for blood, obeying command
Finish the job, destroy them

They came, out of the sea
Unarmed, an armada of hope
Wave after wave, a tide of humanity:
The little ships
Unstoppable, determined
Into wave after wave of mines and bombs
Tearing through flesh, destroying lives

From a sea, red with blood,
They brought hope, salvation:
The little ships
Through a barrage of death
They steamed, wave after wave

Determined, never to give in, never to fail
For the sake of Mankind

Toward the thin spidery lines of broken souls
They surged, to rescue the Tommies
From the jaws of Hell
They saw the job to be done
The prize to be won
The wrong to be undone:

The little ships...
They conquered

—

(Wednesday, 5th September 2018)

THE TRIAL
(a poem in six parts)

I. 1939: The Prelude.

We British are a funny lot
We stand in queues
We moan a lot
If it's not too cold
It's too darned hot by far
A game of darts
A pint or two
A Bob each way
The same for you
Sorry Guv, that's just the way we are
We don't quite stand out in a crowd
We'd rather sit and laugh aloud
Until our back is up against the wall
Have a laugh, have a song
But if old Gerry comes along
We know he'll be heading for a fall
    People call us lazy
    People say we're fools
    We feed the hand that bites us
    We lay it by the rules
    People turn away from us
    When things are going right
    They don't forget which way to turn
    At the first sign of a fight
We British are a funny lot
We stand in queues
We moan a lot

If it's not too cold
It's too darned hot by far
Mister Hitler
Stuff your Reich!
Sorry, Adolf
On yer bike!
Thanks a lot
But we'll just keep
Our crown.

II. 1940: The Evacuation.

Trapped like rats in a barrel, cut off by the sea
A third of a million souls in the jaws of Hell
Strafed, bombed, blasted
On the barren dunes, their hope deserting them
Replaced by death and destruction
Unleashed from Stukas, Messerschmitts
Never again, to look upon the faces of their loved ones, friends

As the end drew near
*"Where is the fu***** RAF?"*
And as they cursed, the Spitfires and Hurricanes
Invisible, inland
Held back the might of the Fatherland:
Baying for blood, obeying command
Finish the job, destroy them

They came out of the sea
Unarmed, an armada of hope
Wave after wave, a tide of humanity:

The little ships
Unstoppable, determined
Into wave after wave of mines and bombs
Tearing through flesh, destroying lives

From a sea, red with blood,
They brought hope, salvation:
The little ships
Through a barrage of death
They steamed, wave after wave
Determined, never to give in, never to fail
For the sake of Mankind

Toward the thin spidery lines of broken souls
They surged, to rescue the Tommies
From the jaws of Hell
They saw the job to be done
The prize to be won
The wrong to be undone:

The little ships...
They conquered

III. 1940: The Backlash.

In 1940 when Hitler's greed
Had terrorised Europe at breath-taking speed
Into each country the Nazi had pushed
Poland had fallen, resistance was crushed
France lay in ruins, Scandinavia raped
Wherever the eagle flew nobody escaped

When Britain refused the Fuhrer's demands
And held out alone against Hitler's commands
The fate of our nation nobody could tell
Nobody could see such a blistering Hell
Would become the result of his temper's eruption
He put Britain next on the list of destruction
He called his chief marshals to draw up a plan
Of how he could quickly take over our land
The date was set, the invasion was nearing
The honour was given to Air Reichsmarshall Goering
To demolish our airfields in the path of a blitz
From Dorniers, Heinkels and Messerschmitts

With our air force in ruins our defence would be lost
The eagle would drop on its prey unopposed
After the Luftwaffe would come the invasion
For Goering had promised yet on this occasion
He had not reckoned on Dowding's young men
Or the devastating punch of Mitchell's gem

On the tenth of July the raids began
Coming over the Channel the radar could scan
A large cloud approaching our Southern shores:
Enemy aircraft arriving in scores
Their deep-throated droning had captured the air
All Britain stood silent, united in prayer

For the impatient young pilots, the order was "*Scramble*»
The fighters took off on their greatest gamble
For to win this battle every trick must be used
But they could not win - yet dare not lose

Into the heavens they raced one by one
To surprise their attackers from out of the sun

Spitfires, Hurricanes - any plane that flew
All went up for the nation knew
That should we fail now in our darkest hour
The Hun would be waiting, ready to devour
Our towns and our cities - all would be smitten
And rubble would lie where once stood Great Britain

Twisting and turning, machine guns loud
Bringing death and destruction from out of each cloud
Rapidly climbing then into a dive
A swarm of angry bees protecting their hive
"Red leader, to green. Red leader, to green
Bandit on you tail. Bandit on your tail"
Fighting and dying, no spirit to lull
Like terriers snapping at the heels of a bull

But just when we thought we had driven them back
They'd return twice as strong in fiercer attack
Wave after wave casting shadows of death
As young pilots burned the world held its breath
Hopelessly outnumbered by five to one
The magnificent "Few" bravely fought on

Clawing at devils became our plight
Screaming defiance became our delight
Three thousand Swastika-clad aircraft
The might of the Fatherland's Luftwaffe
Where murdering our loved ones and destroying our homes
On our island of freedom, the dice had been thrown.

IV. 1941: The Defiance.

Hitler,
Adolf Hitler
You psychopathic god
Do your best to break us
But it won't be good enough
Send your Luftwaffe over
Raining bombs galore
For our island fortress must be crushed
Or you have lost the war.
Try your best to break us
Bring us to our knees
Drive us underneath the ground
Destroy this Bulldog Breed
Do your best to break us
Make the going tough
Try your best to break our hearts and souls
But it won't be near enough
    Cos, we'll all pull together
    Oh, we'll all pull together
    Yes, we'll all pull together
    In this tug of war

    Oh, we'll all pull together
    Yes, we'll all pull together
    Like we've just never done before
Though the world is dark and lonely
Our beacon still shines bright
But, we fear that we're the only ones

To put paid to the march of the Reich
So, we'll all pull together
Oh, we'll all pull together
§ Like we've just never done before
"My old uncle 'enry had a pair of pearly gates
Twenty foot wide, five higher
Til one day he got a letter, taking them away
Now, they're in the wings of a Spitfire!"
Cos we'll all pull together
Oh, we'll all pull together
Like we've just never done before.
"My mother put in front of me
A meal what looked so meek:
One egg, one slice of bacon
I thought what a bloomin' cheek
And when I pulled my mother up
Her voice began to peak:
MEAL? That ain't no meal
My darlin' mother daintily murmured
"THAT'S TO LAST YOU ALL THIS WEEK!"

Cos, we'll all pull together
Oh, we'll all pull together
Yes, we'll all pull together
In this tug of war
Oh, we'll all pull together
Yes, we'll all pull together
Like we've just never done before
Though the world is dark and lonely
Can we see a distant light?
Does the wild Atlantic's awesome roar
Conceal a fearsome bite?

America...
America...
America...

V. 1944: The Deliverance.

They came out of the sea, crashing ashore
Wave after wave, a tide of humanity
Unstoppable, Determined
Into wave after wave of bombs and bullets
Tearing through flesh, destroying young lives
From a sea red with blood, across bloodstained sands
They charged

Wave after wave, determined
Never to give in, never to fail
For the sake of Mankind
To destroy the evil within
They saw the job in hand, across the sand
Of hedgehogs, barbed wire, a million mines
Rommel's wall destined to fall.

They dropped out of the sky, by the thousand
A torrent of courage, a storm of humanity
Unstoppable, determined, into a sea of fire
Across blood-drenched fields, they charged
Wave after wave, determined
Never to give in, never to fail
For the sake of Mankind

To drive the evil within

Back to the gates of Berlin
They saw the job to be done
The prize to be won
The wrong to be undone
They conquered

VI. 1945: The End.

Beneath the soil
In foreign fields
At rest, the young men lie
Caressed by the wind
Blessed by the sun
Forever, to face the sky
How long will we appreciate
The sacrifice they gave
In handing us our freedom
As they marched to an early grave?
Young lads, young men
All as one
Of laughter and of tears
Of broken hearts
Of beer and darts
All wrapped in tender years
Of football, sweethearts, motorbikes
The innocence of the young
Torn from their grasp
By the wail of death
No more, their song to be sung

How long will we remember them

And the sacrifice they made?
In granting us our future
It can never be repaid

Beneath gravestones
Far from their homes
In death, the young men lie
Row upon row
Upon row
Upon row
Forever, to face the sky.

——

THIS POPPY

You will not grow this poppy
In carefully tended soil
Or gently weeded borders
So, do not waste your toil
Put away your gardening tools
Your spade, your fork, your rake
Do not waste your fancy pots
By making this mistake

Believing you will cultivate
This gracefully nodding plant
To show off to your neighbours
For your payment will be scant
Put away your fancy thoughts
You'll work for no reward
Do not waste the daydreams
That will never strike a chord

You will not grow this poppy
In carefully tended soil
Or gently weeded borders
So, do not waste your toil
This poppy grows in No-Man's Land
Its soil disturbed in tons
Instead of water, pour on blood
From the wrath of a thousand guns

For fertilizer, feed it bones
And from death, life will spring
A swathe of vermillion, scarlet, crimson

To camouflage mankind's sins
A blanket of red now comforts we dead
Us long-forgotten lads
Lost in action to the merciless guns:
Husbands, brothers, sons, and dads

—

(Saturday, 27th October 2018)

In memory of all those lost in action, who never received the dignity of a grave.

WE BRITISH

We British are a funny lot
We stand in queues
We moan a lot
If it's not too cold
It's too darned hot by far
A game of darts
A pint or two
A Bob each way
The same for you
Sorry Guv, that's just the way we are

We don't quite stand out in a crowd
We'd rather sit and laugh aloud
Until our back is up against the wall
Have a laugh, have a song
But if old Gerry comes along
We know he'll be heading for a fall

People call us lazy
People say we're fools
We feed the hand that bites us
We lay it by the rules
People turn away from us
When things are going right
They don't forget which way to turn
At the first sign of a fight

We British are a funny lot
We stand in queues
We moan a lot

If it's not too cold
It's too darned hot by far
Mister Hitler
Stuff your Reich!
Sorry, Adolf
On yer bike!
Thanks a lot
But we'll just keep
Our crown

—

(Written in 1983)

WORLD WAR 1: TRILOGY

(written for the 100th anniversary of the 1918 Armistice)

(I): PALS

They were not soldiers' those who went
Happily, off to war
Pals together toward their deaths
From the horror that lay in store
Of slaughter from the starving guns
None of this foreseen
By the *'Pals Battalions'* from the cobbled streets
To the glorious fields of green

They were the volunteer army
'Lord Kitchener Wants You'
The poster said patriotically
As the clarion bugles blew
And so, the call was answered
By the thousands signing up
To taste the Devil's banquet
And sip from the poisoned cup

The fresh, the young, the gullible
All swallowed Rawlinson's ruse
Convinced that they were soldiers
And eager to pay their dues
Friends and colleagues' side by side
Through the flaming gates of Hell
As the generals played their heartless games
The friends and colleagues' fell
They were not soldiers' those who went

Marching to the Somme
The Marne or Ypres or Amiens
Just Britain's naive sons
Busmen, binmen, labourers
Dying shoulder to shoulder
You can put a uniform onto a man
But that doesn't make him a soldier

—

(Written: Tuesday, 30th October 2018)

"I remember when the news came through to Accrington that the Pals had been wiped out. I don't think there was a street in Accrington and district that didn't have their blinds drawn, and the bell at Christ Church tolled all day."
Percy Holmes, the brother of one of the Pals, remembers what happened when the soldiers from Accrington didn't return home.

(II): OVER THE TOP
(inspired by the poetry of Wilfred Owen)

We crouched like diseased tramps racked with pain.
Young Tom crying in fear.
Harry, vomiting violently into the mud.
Some mumbling through half-forgotten prayers, as if there was a God.
Others stared like corpses, with premonitions of the ugliness to come.
The only ones who had any semblance of sense among that Hell of madness were the rats

who scurried from scrap to scrap, oblivious to the fate, of their superior beings.

'Ready lads!' He shouted as if we were going on a jolly jaunt.
Seconds later the whistles blew.
Up the ladders we surged.
Out of the trench.
Over the top.

Roaring with false bravado we charged
toward the roaring relentless clatter of the guns.
They began dropping around me. Young Tom copped it first.
I made it a hundred yards before I was hit.
One took off my left ear, another burst through my jugular
the third straight through my ribs and into the top of my lung.
The force sent me spinning into a shell crater.
I landed on my front then managed to roll over before losing consciousness.
And there, in that crater, my life came to an end as I choked
on vomit and blood.
I was twenty-two.
For me it was over.
For thousands more, until the Armistice,
it was about to begin.

(Written: Sunday, 23rd September 2018)

(III): THIS POPPY

(In memory of all those lost in action, who never received the dignity of a grave.)

You will not grow this poppy
In carefully tended soil
Or gently weeded borders
So do not waste your toil
Put away your gardening tools
Your spade your fork your rake
Do not waste your fancy pots
By making this mistake

Believing you will cultivate
This gracefully nodding plant
To show off to your neighbours
For your payment will be scant
Put away your fancy thoughts
You'll work for no reward
Do not waste the daydreams
That will never strike a chord

You will not grow this poppy
In carefully tended soil
Or gently weeded borders
So do not waste your toil
This poppy grows in No-Man's Land
Its soil disturbed in tons
Instead of water pour on blood
From the wrath of a thousand guns

For fertilizer feed it bones
And from death life will spring
A swathe of vermillion scarlet crimson
To camouflage mankind's sins
A blanket of red now comforts we dead
Us, long-forgotten lads
Lost in action to the merciless guns
Husbands, brothers, sons, and dads

—

(Written: Saturday, 27th October 2018)

Warranty Claims!

(naïve poems from a past life)

A BITTER ROSE

There is no scent more fragrant
than the scent of revenge

No petal is more fragile
than the petal of deceit

There is no stem more twisted
than a liar's tongue

No thorn is as sharp
as the thorn of jealousy

There are no roots that grow deeper
than the roots of hatred

Within us all
can grow a bitter rose

And there is no flower
more difficult to prune

—

(circa 1968-1973)

A CHANGEABLE LOT

He rode through the streets
On the back of an ass
They showered his path
With palm leaves and grass
A bearded man of about thirty-five
With love in his heart
But pain in his eyes
With each word he spoke
The crowd went wild
But they were a changeable lot

He passed quite close
He was dusty and tanned
A saviour they said
From a far-off land
The children sang and danced in the streets
The women fought to wash his feet
Even the menfolk were standing agog
But they were a changeable lot

In a gentle voice he spoke of love
And peace on earth and a father, above
They would have believed, but for the scribes
And Pharisees with their trumped-up lies
And distracting tongues and mocking jibes
For they were a changeable lot

At the end of the week with a spear in his side
And a crown made of thorns, he was crucified
A few of them laughed and a few of them cried
Because they were a changeable lot.

(written circa 1968-78)

ALL THE WHALES ARE DEAD

A gentle giant of the sea
Disembowelled for you and me
To spread upon our morning toast
Will no one save this fading ghost?

I fell asleep and had a dream
And watched the oceans turning red
And as I dreamed, the fulmars screamed
"All the whales are dead.
All the whales are dead"

I waded out and waded forth
Until my legs had turned to rubber
Then realised that where I stood
Was a sea of floating blubber
As overhead the cry was heard
"All the whales are dead.
All the whales are dead."
Oh! silent monster of the deep
A speck of dust in the universe
What will the cleaners find to sweep?
When the last of your breed has gone
When the last of your breed has gone

(circa 1968-1973)

ANDREW
(FIRST BORN)

If I could choose in all the world
From everything that I have ever loved
Then you would be the one, my son
You would be the one

And if I had to take my choice
From every smile that I had ever seen
Then yours would be the smile I'd choose
For yours is part of me

If I stood in the ruins of a life
With only the ashes of an existence
To show for all that I had ever owned
As long as I had you, my son,
Then I would still be standing proud

If I could choose in all the world
From everything that I had ever loved
Then you would be the one, my son
You would be the one

(Written 1974)

CHICHESTER'S RETURN

One day while sitting on a boulder
Pulling petals off a sea daisy
I looked out into the ocean

In the distance if I screwed my eyes up
I could see a tiny sailing boat
As it grew closer, I could see a man

He looked very lonely, so I waved
He waved back and seemed pleased
I hope he was

Gypsy... something – no.
I couldn't quite make out the name
Of that tiny sailing boat

—

(Circa: 1968-1978)

An imaginary sighting of Sir Francis Chichester as he reached home after his single circumnavigation of the world in the boat 'Gypsy Moth IV'.

CHRISTMAS DAY, 1974

No snow, no ice
No tears, no rice
No heat, no steam
No drawn-out stream
Of moans and groans
'cause this is Christmas Day

Sun and fun!
Sherry and pies!
Hats and tails!
Seltzer and wails!
On Christmas Day.

No living death
No dying life
No clinging mud
No dripping blood

No bombs
No bullets
Until tomorrow

Even the IRA
Like a day off.

(written on Christmas Day 1974)

EAGLE

Eagle
Master of the Highland sky
Perched on a throne of granite rock
How does it feel to breathe fresh air
Gliding alone above the loch
Far from the hungry guns of Man
A distant speck in Heaven's eye
Closer to God than to the glen
Master of the Highland sky

—

(Written circa 1968-1978)

GHOST

Upon the deep and gla-zed pool
That coats a wardrobe's rich veneer
Each night at twelve without a fail
A death-white ghost-like face appears

With sunken eyes and gaping mouth
As if straight from the grave
Its vacant stare and murmured breath
Would chill the very brave

Across the room it slowly shifts
No harm to me does it imply
Yet still it lingers on the air
A melancholic passer-bye

Unloved unwanted daunted thing
That tries in vain to me to speak
Yet fails each time and turns away
Into the night, its sullen cheek

(written circa: 1968-1978)

HOMELESS

I saw an old man on a bench in the park
Lying in slumber, his eyebrows were dark
His nostrils were hairy, his forehead was creased
Quietly snoring, his world was at peace

A bundle of treasures placed under his head
A cloth cap, an orange, a loaf of stale bread
Under the oak tree, his white beard, damp
Was he a wizard, a king, or a tramp?

Where had he come from, where was he aimed?
He wasn't bothered, they're both just the same
Deaf to the noise from the geese on the lake
Silently dreaming of onions and steak

Could he enjoy it, existing alone?
A King without knights on a make-believe throne
Moving along, always one step ahead
Wherever the night fell – there was his bed

Had he a mother, a wife or a friend?
There must have been somebody willing to lend
A hand to him when he was hungry or scared
Surely, there must have been someone who cared?

I saw an old man on a bench in the park
On that cold afternoon, the beginning of March
Stiffened and damp by the blustery roar
The old man on the bench will awaken no more

—

('The Tramp' originally written 1970s. Re-written as 'Homeless')
Thursday, 11th January 2018

INNOCENCE

(Scouse accent)

Me mam said t'tell y' she's norrin
An' if y' the rentman
She's not gunna pay y'
Til yuv fixed them slates on deroof
Cos wennit rains de bedroom gets flooded
Anwe avte purra bucket under deole
T'catch d' water

An me mam said tha'
If y' de tellyman
Welli' duzzen marrer now
Cos me dad took the backoff

An me mam said tha'
If y' the windacleaner
Y'missed de backs out again lassweek
An' y' wannatry doin' the lobby winda
If it's not too much trouble

An' me mam said tha'
Ifyeh me uncle Charlie
Whose cumin t'fix the wardrobe door
Welta go right up
Cos me dad's on nights this week

An me mam said tharram
not t'tell anyonelse
worrav justole you...
Can you tell me the way to Smithdown Road, please son?

——

(written circa: 1968-1978)

OLD McDONALD

Old McDonald had a farm
Ee aye ee aye o!

And on that farm, he
Butchered all the animals
Turned them into beefburgers
Then sold them through his
Fast food chain
Eee aye ee aye o!

With a ching ching here
And a ching ching there
Here a ching, there a ching
Everywhere a ching ching
Old McDonald's tills overflowed
Eee aye ee aye o!

—

(Sunday, 2nd December 2012)

PRISONERS' THREE

Gone – the swaying thistle heads
the groundsel fronds and chickweed beds
the once-proud chest of scarlet red
from the linnet in its cage
no more – the sun upon it's back
it's golden song the wind will lack
a forgotten member of the flock
trapped in a tiny cage

Forward and backward
round and around
backward and forward
pacing the ground
a spite-filled snarl on his whiskered face
far from Bengal in deep disgrace
a thorn in his side named The Human Race
restlessly pacing the ground

Into the dungeon dark and deep
where many a man has feared to tread
nightly we file as if in sleep
for our minds have long been dead
away from the laughing sounds of earth
far from the setting sun
into each tomb for what it's worth
until our toil is done

—

(circa 1977-1981, the second stint)

Inspired by the mind-numbing drudgery of working 10-hour night shifts in Ford's.

REINA DEL MAR

What phantom haunts the Mersey's swirling mist?
What mirage sails the river's sullen depths?
That bids farewell a yearning such is this
Condemned to watch from these moss-covered steps.

She steams toward the distant, hidden bar
And turns her back on England's choking smog
In search of new horizons of afar
She slowly disappears into the fog

Toward the wild Atlantic's awesome roar
She aims in haste to find a warmer day
She has no fear to leave this sheltered shore
For as she sails, a halcyon, guides her way

To anchor off a Caribbean coast
Or rest within a peaceful blue lagoon
Beneath the stars, a glinting silver ghost
She sleeps beneath Tahiti's golden moon

Leaving me behind to play the fool
And trudge the cobbled streets
of Liverpool

(Original poem, written 1964, since rewritten as a folk ballad, inspired by seeing the Reina Del Mar at anchor, mid-river, in a foggy Mersey, one January afternoon)

RUSTY

Two dozen tins of Heinz chicken soup
Once filled the box that is now your home
A bottle-green jumper with ragged sleeves
Keeps you alive as you sleep alone

But turn again, Rusty, and never look back
From a rag and bone start there is nothing you will lack
Except the affection a mother would show
To her furry young offspring
As well you know

What is it Rusty? You are restless tonight
Are you missing your mother, as well you might

Never mind, Rusty, keep fighting on
When the crisis is over, and the battle is won
Like the tiger who owns the forest he stalks
Then, little Rusty, all this will be yours

(written circa 1973)

Written about a tiny, marmalade Tom kitten that I 'rescued' from my niece, Anne. His eyes were still not fully open, and she'd been given him by her friend, whose dad had told her to dispose of their cat's litter of kittens or he would drown them. I fed him with milk from an eye dropper, and he gradually began to pull through. The first night, he cried persistently for his mother.

ODE TO THE ROLLS-ROYCE SILVER SHADOW

She floats like a morning mist so thin
Through a sleeping valley to within
The forest pines so thick and low
As silent as her name would show
For silence, is the Shadow

A distant muted silken purr
So quiet to deceive the ear
As the nightly owl sweeps through the dell
She passes close yet none can tell
So quiet is the Shadow

Her lissom body lithe and low
Pure as a mountain's virgin snow
Pale as a moonlight-shrouded birch
A glistening opalescent pearl
So gentle is the shadow

Cast in the same superior mould
As Phantom Wraith and Ghost of old
The flying lady trails her gown
For all to see yet none shall frown
So precious is the Shadow

(written circa: 1968-1978)
At the time, my favourite car.

SUFFER, THE LITTLE CHILDREN

Suffer, the little children
That come unto me
For such is the Kingdom of Heaven

And yours was a typical case, little Wayne
For where you are now
You will feel no more pain

There will be no more beatings
You will shed no more tears
Asleep in the arms of Jesus

Father, forgive

(circa: 1968-1973)

Inspired by the newspaper story of a toddler named Wayne, who was systematically beaten by his stepfather, until eventually the boy died.

THE CREEP

He clasps his pen with crooked hands
Far from the sun in dusty lands
Ringed by the typing pool he stands
Behind the thick and laden walls
The hatchet-waving monster bawls
And like a thunderbolt
He crawls.

—

(Written circa 1968-1978)

Inspired by an office, work colleague.

After Alfred, Lord Tennyson:

THE EAGLE

He clasps the crag with crooked hands;

Close to the sun in lonely lands,

Ring'd with the azure world, he stands.

The wrinkled sea beneath him crawls;

He watches from his mountain walls,

And like a thunderbolt he falls.

—

THE FOREST

She fell upon the sodden earth that lay between the trees and stream half buried in the soaking moss toward the sylvan screen she crawled her bulging eyes astir to find the cave where, as a child she played without a care - across the slippery jagged rocks and past the dripping ferns - then to the left – *or was it right?* - her tortured mind could not recall the varied hidden turns.
For three long days and endless nights her burning lungs had screamed in vain she dared not
rest for fear she might be trapped and caged again and now amid the forest's peace shared
only with a singing bird the haunting wail of man and beast no longer could be heard.

Beneath the dancing... gurgling foam
that swirled around the river's edge...
amidst the weaving weeds and stones
that formed a sheltered ledge...
in deep recluse, from a turmoiled world
that swallows all who dare to pause
in silent bliss... beneath the flood...
a sleeping trout at rest...
No twisted thought, no worried mind,
harassed that sleeping trout...
Upon the current, in and out
Of soothing shade and warming light...
The large and lazy trout reclined...
its movements... smooth...
and... slow...

—

(Re-written from 'The Fugitive / The Sleeping Trout')
Tuesday, 11th September 2018

THE MILKMAN

"Two pints, please..." read the milkman
through blood-stained eyes
neatly printed on the back
of a Bill Taylor betting slip
the words that is – not the blood-stained eyes

though it's hard to tell when your head's banging
and the wind's whistling 'God Save the Queen'
down your ears
and you're running around waiting on people
who won't be awake for another three hours'
and you've run out of yoghurt
ah, well – roll on death
and let's get to Hell out of here
roll on tonight, and let's get back on the beer.

—

(Circa: 1968-1978)

Inspired by a friend who used to be a milkman.

THE RAVEN'S MEAL

He sits and waits, the prince of the ravine
In his granite castle, high above the scree
His eye is sharp, his heart is cold
He sits majestically
Above, the kestrel's ghostlike flight
Below, the Aled's roar
Cannot distract his piercing look
From the lamb on the snow-clad moor

In the cold grey light of a frozen morn
Amongst the heather stems
Lying alone on the frigid ground
A lamb, devoid of friends
"Lie still. Lie still, my new-born son
The raven is at hand
Lie still, lie still until your legs
Have found the strength to stand"

But his mother's words have been ignored
The impatient lamb has moved
Betraying Nature's camouflage
The hunter's skill has been proved
On outstretched wings of glistening black
Slowly circling down
Gliding from his rocky throne
The shadow of death on the prowl

With gleaming eye and sharpened bill
The raven gently lands
Upon the glistening powdered snow

Where the tiny victim's strand of life
Is quickly wearing thin
Unable to bleat for his mother's help
Only the howling moorland wind
Will mourn the wretched whelp

Mercy is an unknown word
To the executioner of the moor
But the kill will be swift and quickly done
For that is Nature's law
With a dazzling flash of a glossy beak
The lamb's eye is plucked from its head
A tasty morsel for the raven's young
As the new-born lamb lies dead

Taking to the air, riding the wind
Down the Welsh ravine
The raven gloats over its precious find
Not knowing that it has been seen
By an angry shepherd's lad
Who fires his gun at the raven's heart
In the cold, grey light of a frozen morn
The raven's young began to starve

—

(circa 1968)

THE TALE OF THE MERSEY QUEEN

When I was just a young boy
At a very precious age
I fell in love with the river ferry
As we left the landing stage
She captured my affection
And the love I had to share
Her mighty engines thundered
As we headed who knows where

She was the fastest pirate ship
The world had ever seen
I raised the Jolly Roger
And I named her Mersey Queen
She was the sleekest whaler
That ever put to sail
And I was Captain Ahab
Searching for the giant whale

We fought the fearsome oceans
And we sailed the Seven Seas
And single-handed beat the Horn
The Mersey Queen and me
We brought home silk from China
And bars of gold from Spain
Then when my tuppence had run out
We put to sea again

And now I stand and watch her
As she ferries back and forth
Remembering times that we enjoyed

Such things that can't be bought
No more, a ransom on our heads
No more, the natives wild
No more, is she my Mersey Queen...
No more, am I a child

(Originated as a poem, circa: 1968.
Re-written as a simple, Liverpool folk ballad 27th June 2017)

THOROUGHLY MODERN MOTHER

Born to this world
Born and brought up
Without ever knowing a mother's love

Back to work
Back to work
The mortgage has got to be paid

Back to work
Back to work
Majorca has got to be made

—

(written circa: 1968-1978)

THOUGHT

I have never seen the world nor craved to
I have never bought the moon or saved to
Beauty lies not on four wheels
But upon the corn in a harvest field
Or upon the leaves in an autumn glad
Not cut and stitched and tailor-made

I pity the man who can see no further than his wallet
For when its contents have gone
He shall find loneliness in more ways than one

(written circa: 1968-1978)

TO JO AND TERRY – A FOND FAREWELL

(two married friends, emigrating to New Zealand)

If you both knew as much as I
How much I want you both to stay
Then you would never say goodbye
And you would never go away

These past few months our friendship has grown
From a tiny seedling freshly sown
Into an ivy-covered tree
Entwining both of you to me

So, spare a thought when far away
To the happy times that we have spent
These past few months from day to day
The last few months before you went

If you both knew as much as I
How much I want you both to stay
Then you would never say goodbye
For you would never go away.

—

(written circa: 1972-73)

TO NELSON, DREAMING AT THE FIRESIDE

There lies the lowly mongrel dog
Beside the fire, bright
Where cracks a blazing hawthorn log
As onward draws the night
The burning heat his forehead scorch
The flying spark his chest to sting
He will not move 'til daybreak's torch
Has woken up the earth

A ruffled twisted hungry face
Close to the ground he lies in sleep
One more night he has earned his place
Close to his master's feet
His nostrils twitch, his eyelids stir
Lost in a land of open fields
Racing the wind to catch a hare
Lost in a world of dreams

For this short time his chores are none
No watchdog duty has he now
He is a greyhound – watch him fly
A speeding arrow from the bow
There is no man to shout him down
To make him bend or change his will
Only the frightened fleeing hare
He worries down the hill

This tiny one-eyed faithful beast
Companion of my heart
Whimpering softly in his rest

As now he runs, apart
A sudden yelp, a nervous jump
Alone he spurts in chase
That private land is his domain
There, reigns no human face

—

(written circa: 1968-1978)

A romanticised poem about 'Nelson', a mongrel dog owned by George & Mary Hirons, my father and mother-in-law.

WANDERLUST

(to Meg, a Labrador dog)

Let us away to the rolling moor
Where sounds the curlew's mourn-filled cry
Where sings the lark from Heaven's door
Beyond the lonely sky
To wind through tousled cotton grass
Across the valley's breast
Onto the peat-stained, reed-swelled marsh
To flush the redshank from her nest

Come Meg, away to the sun-flecked wood
In search of peaceful solitude
Wherein the twisted bracken deep
The woodcock hides her brood
To sit and watch the mottled sunlight
Soak into the earth
Until the fading light of day
Will sound of nightjar's mirth

Let us away to the howling shore
To plod the windswept shifting dunes
And hear the echo coming home
Of restless pipers' tunes
We two, shall roam that lonely land
And watch the morning rise
Where salt winds blow, and campions grow
Beneath the frozen sky

Come Meg, let us away

—

(circa 1968-73)

A poem about my imaginary dog.

And finally, a handful of songs...

EVERYTIME

Verse 1:
People tell me I'm a fool for loving you
That no good will ever come from what you do.
And deep inside my heart I must agree
I just can't see a future here for me
People tell me that I'm wrong in loving you
But I know I must be strong although it's true
For deep inside my heart I live a lie
I just can't see, the reason why...

Chorus:
Everytime... everytime... everytime I think of you
Even though the things you do tear me apart
Everytime... everytime... everytime I see your face
I just know I can't replace you in my heart.

Verse 2:
People talk behind my back and laugh at me
All my friends say I am blind and cannot see
I know it's hard for them to understand
The feeling that I get each time you hold my hand
People talk and say I'll pay for my mistake
That I do all the give and you do all the take
But I know that they will never see
That look within your eyes that starts the fire in me...

Closing chorus:
Everytime... everytime... everytime I think of you... (etc.)

HERO OF LIVERPOOL

Verse 1:
Back in the fifties' this city of ours
Didn't have much going on
We needed a hero, we searched for a star
But Macca had only met John
And our dear old Doddy was just starting out
There was nobody to fit the bill
Then out of the shadows - a giant emerged
At the bottom of Copperas Hill

Verse 2:
He was such a big fellow (in more ways than one)
From the top of his head to his feet
And all the Scouse Judies who rushed to say "hello"
Caused chaos in Ranelagh Street
We'd never seen anything like him before
Liverpool all stood agog
This naked young giant with muscles of bronze
(And something that looked like a log)

Chorus (to the tune of 'Daisy, Daisy'):
Dickie, Dickie, hero of Liverpool
We're so proud, la, we all look up to you
We just don't know how you've stuck it
Where the cleaner hangs her bucket
You'll make a splash in Knotty Ash
If you ever decide to move

Verse 3:
And now since the fifties', big Dickie is known

The length and the breadth of the world
In every far corner where his fame has grown
Our Liverpool flag has unfurled
And everyone wants him, but he's always been ours
Ever since that first day he came forth
'We all love big Dickie' the Judies still sing
Dear Dickie – our Cock of the North

Chorus:
Dickie, Dickie, hero of Liverpool
We're so proud, la, we all look up to you
We just don't know how you've stuck it
Where the cleaner hangs her bucket
You'll make a splash in Knotty Ash
If you ever decide to move...

Repeat chorus

—

(Originated as a one-verse ditty, to the tune of 'Daisy, Daisy', circa: 1995.)
Re-written as a Liverpool comedy tribute to Dickie Lewis:

Thursday, 22nd June 2017

LIVERPOOL

Verse 1:
Liverpool, my Liverpool
So silently you lie
Beside the Mersey, deep and cool
And watch the ships go by
Whenever I am far away
And feeling so forlorn
My thoughts return to Liverpool
The place where I was born

Verse 2:
I have walked your broken streets
And darkened alleyways
I have crawled your gutters
When my mind was in a haze
And still you cast your spell on me
With the feelings you impart
You're still the one who holds the key
To the gateway of my heart

(musical interlude)

Verse 3:
And ever since a little child
So many years ago
When smiles, then tears, then laughter
Became my ebb and floe
Each time life tried to knock me down
With your blood in my veins
When all those tears had disappeared

Your laughter, still remained

Bridge:

Liverpool... my mistress by the sea
Liverpool... my soul lies deep in thee
Liverpool... will you ever hear my plea?
Liverpool... will you ever set me free...?

Closing chorus:

Liverpool, my Liverpool
So silently you lie
Beside the Mersey, deep and cool
And watch the ships go by
And now that I am far away
And feeling so forlorn
My thoughts return to Liverpool
The place where I was born...

My thoughts return to Liverpool
The place where I was born...

My thoughts return... to Liverpool...
The place... where... I... was...
born.

(First eleven lines originated circa: 1968-1978, as a fragment of poem, then dormant until Friday, 23rd June 2017, when re-written and completed as a Liverpool folk ballad. Unperformed.

LIZZIE

Opening chorus:
Lizzie, always thinking of you
Lizzie, can't stop thinking of you
Now, that you're gone
Don't you know
I'm the one who misses you
Lizzie, my heart is breaking for you
Lizzie, can't stop aching for you
Now, that you're gone
Don't you know
I'm the one who's missing you

Verse 1:
Lizzie went away
One cold September day
When the clouds were hanging frozen
To the sky
She just went away
She didn't even say
Now my heart is broken
I know why
That I sing

Chorus 2:
Lizzie, always thinking of you
Lizzie, can't stop thinking of you
Now, that you're gone
Don't you know
I'm the one who misses you
Lizzie, my heart is breaking for you

Lizzie, can't stop aching for you
Now, that you're gone
Don't you know
I'm the one who's missing you

Verse 2:
One day she'll return
I know my heart will yearn
Until the day I see her
Coming home
Maybe then she'll see
How much she means to me
But until that day
I'll stand alone
And I'll sing

Closing chorus:
Lizzie, always thinking of you
Lizzie, can't stop thinking of you
Now, that you're gone
Don't you know
I'm the one who misses you
Lizzie, my heart is breaking for you
Lizzie, can't stop aching for you
Now, that you're gone
Don't you know
I'm the one who's missing you
Now

—

I wrote this naïve song in my early teens. My mother Elizabeth 'Lizzie' Jones died on Sunday, 27th September 1959. She was forty-seven years old. I was eleven.

REINA DEL MAR

(Queen of the Sea)

Verse 1:

What phantom haunts the Mersey's swirling mist?
What mirage sails the river's sullen depths?
That bids farewell a yearning such is this
Condemned to watch from these moss-covered steps.
She steams toward the distant, hidden bar
And turns her back on England's choking smog
In search of new horizons of afar
She slowly disappears into the fog

Verse 2:

Toward the wild Atlantic's open door
She aims with grace to find a warmer day
She has no fear to leave this sheltered shore
For as she sails, the stars will guide her way
To anchor off a Caribbean coast
To rest within a peaceful blue lagoon
Beneath the stars, a glinting silver ghost
She'll sleep beneath Tahiti's golden moon

(musical interlude)

Bridge:

A vision of beauty, she moves from the quay
This pale gleaming spectre bids farewell to me
Our journey together was not meant to be
Goodbye, my dear lady, my Queen of the Sea

Closing chorus:

What phantom haunts the Mersey's swirling mist?
What mirage sails the river's sullen depths?
That bids farewell a yearning such is this
Condemned to watch from these moss-covered steps
She steams toward the distant, hidden bar
And turns her back on England's choking smog
In search of new horizons of afar
She slowly disappears into the fog...

Leaving me behind to play the fool
And walk the cobbled streets...
of Liverpool

—

(Originally written as a four-verse poem in1964. Inspired by an actual sighting of the Reina Del Mar, anchored mid-river in the foggy Mersey, January 1964. Re-written as a Liverpool folk ballad, 26th June 2017. Remains unperformed.)

THAT GIRL!

(a thumping, 1950's-style, rock & roll number)

The drums start a pounding, intro beat.
The singer appeals to the audience (tongue-in-cheek)
Singer:
c'mon – clap your feet... stamp your hands...
(jokingly) empathise with me... because –
Big drum build-up to...

Opening chorus:
That girl is driving me mad...
That girl is driving me mad...
That girl ain't good, she is bad
And that girl is driving me mad
That girl is driving me mad -
She's driving me mad for love!

Repeat chorus:
That girl is driving me mad...
That girl is driving me mad...
That girl ain't good, she is bad
And that girl is driving me mad
That girl is driving me mad -
She's driving me mad for love

Verse 1:
When, I wake up in the mornin'
She is in my bed
I shuffle off to work
And she is in my head
I'm sippin' on my coffee

Like a drunken toad
But then the thought of her
Makes my mind explode
She's got everything I need
To keep me feeling hot
That girl has got the lot...

Repeat chorus:
That girl is driving me mad...
That girl is driving me mad...
That girl ain't good, she is bad
And that girl is driving me mad
That girl is driving me mad -
She's driving me mad for love!

Verse 2:
When I'm climbing up the stairs
On my way to sleep
I feel my eyes a-stingin'
Need to count some sheep
But then the door will open
And she's standing there
At the bottom of the bed
With her flowing hair
And her body that's as smooth
As a velvet glove
I ain't too tired for love!

Repeat chorus:
Because - that girl is driving me mad...
That girl is driving me mad...
That girl ain't good, she is bad

And that girl is driving me mad
That girl is driving me mad -
She's driving me mad for love!

Bridge:
She's so wicked
She's so mad
She makes me happy
She makes me glad
When she's good
She's very good
But when she's bad –
She's better!

Closing chorus:
That girl is driving me mad...
That girl is driving me mad...
That girl ain't good, she is bad
And that girl is driving me mad
That girl is driving me mad -
She's driving me mad for love!
I said, she's driving me mad for love
She's driving me mad for love...
Holy Moly!

——

(Monday, 6th August 2018)

THE SCOUSERS AND THE MANCS

(a comedy/novelty song with audience participation)

Chorus 1:
The Scousers and the Mancs
The Scousers and the Mancs
Ee-aye-addio
The Scousers and the Mancs

All together now!

The Scousers and the Mancs
The Scousers and the Mancs
Ee-aye-addio
The Scousers and the Mancs

Verse 1:

Up in the North-West of England
Where the Cockneys are all scared to go
There's two rival, great, mighty cities
Ruled by football and music, you know

Off to the west, there's the Scousers
Liverpool, loud, hard and proud
Then to the east, there's the Mankies
Manchester, proud, hard and loud

Repeat chorus:
The Scousers and the Mancs
The Scousers and the Mancs
Ee-aye-addio
The Scousers and the Mancs

The Scousers and the Mancs
The Scousers and the Mancs
Ee-aye-addio
The Scousers and the Mancs

Verse 2:

Which one of these is the greatest?
Whichever one you say you will be wrong
One of them smelling of roses
The other one creating a pong

Manchester's the greatest!

"Ar 'ey, y' jokin' aren't y'? Y' Manc Divvie – Liverpool's boss, la - Boss!"

Liverpool's the greatest!

"Madchester – result, sorted, top, mad for it, y' Scouse Tossor!"

Repeat chorus:

The Scousers and the Mancs
The Scousers and the Mancs
Ee-aye-addio
The Scousers and the Mancs

The Scousers and the Mancs
The Scousers and the Mancs
Ee-aye-addio
The Scousers and the Mancs

Verse 3:

How can we solve this conundrum?

Will there ever an answer be found?
Maybe we're two separate branches
Sharing one common root underground

At least we've got one thing in common
We Northerners know how it feels
At the match with a pint and a pasty
So, sod off – you can stuff your jellied eels

Closing chorus:
The Scousers and the Mancs
The Scousers and the Mancs
Ee-ay-addio
The Scousers and the Mancs

The Scousers and the Mancs
The Scousers and the Mancs
Ee-ay-addio
The Scousers and the Mancs

—

(Sunday, 25th June 2017)

Inspired by, and written for, a Manchester United fanatic friend (for his sins).

And finally, a handful of songs...

THE SONGWRITER

(about a songwriter who can't write songs)

Verse 1:

Ev'ry time I write a song
The lyrics turn out wrong
The melody don't 'melod' like it should
So, I tinker with each word
'Til each vowel and note are paired
But the song still ends up sounding like it should... n't

Verse 2:

As I struggle with each syllable
On a blank page - oh so fillable
My mind explodes beneath my thinking cap
Then my heart begins to pound
As I chop and change each sound
'Til... "It's finished!"
Still it ends up sounding - Pap.

Bridge:

Why can't it be me?
Why must it be McCartney?
Why is the kudos not mine?
Instead of that schmuck - Hammerstein?
Mr Porter, what can I do?
I just wanna be like you
Night and Day these pages I'm fillin'
So, God willin', I'll turn out like Dylan

Verse 3:

Ev'ry time I chew my pen

Then chomp an' chew again
The thoughts, emotions, feelings swell inside
As I try to make some sense
It's just no coincidence
That before too long I need another pen

Verse 4:
As I tackle ev'ry verse
Things just go from bad to worse
I sometimes make up words that don't exist
As I try to make them fit
It just sounds a load of – garbage
So, I open up the whisky and get – drunk

Bridge 2:
Deep down in my heart
I wanna be like Lionel Bart
Make that journey from page to stage
That Lloyd Webber fills me with rage
To whom can I turn?
Mr Newley teach me to learn
I just need that break maybe then an'
My songs will be bigger than Lennon...
maybe not

Closing verse:
Ev'ry time I write a song
The lyrics turn out wrong...
As I struggle with each syllable
On a blank page – oh so fillable...
It's increasingly clear to see...
Maybe...

there's no songwriter...
in...
me

—

(circa 2004.)

Printed in Great Britain
by Amazon